Brenda Belmonte

Silky Terriers

Everything About Purchase, Grooming, Health, Nutrition, Care, and Training

Filled with Full-color Photographs

Illustrations by Michele Earle-Bridges

BARRON'S

CONTENTS

SILKY TERRIERS—
IN THE BEGINNING

More than 200 years ago, in the "land down under," experimental pairings of different breeds aimed at improving one breed of dog resulted in the creation of something new—a breed so wonderful, yet different from its previous ancestors—known today as the Silky Terrier.

A Silky History

The Silky Terrier has a fascinating history that spans several centuries. To fully understand the origin of this unique toy dog, it is important to take a glimpse of several other terrier breeds and their histories.

Australian Origins

The Australian Terrier's history is rich with the bloodlines of other terrier ancestors, including some breeds that are no longer in existence. Breeds such as the now extinct Rough Coated Terrier were instrumental in establishing the trademark harsh coat of the Australian Terrier, while other breeds more commonly seen today, such as the Norwich, Cairn, and Scottish Terriers may have played

The Silky Terrier is the perfect fit for many families.

a role in creating the compact size of the Australian Terrier. In the late 1800s, fanciers of the Australian Terrier began a quest to improve the blue and tan coat color of their breed. Serious breeders of the era imported Yorkshire Terriers from England and bred them to their prized Australian Terriers, hoping to intensify and further improve the unique blue and tan color.

Many of these litters produced puppies with mixed coat types and variations in the size of the offspring. Some of the pups closely resembled their Australian Terrier parent. Others were smaller in size, finer in bone, and had longer coats due to the Yorkshire Terrier influence. There was also a third group of puppies, whose size was more moderate than that of the Australian Terrier, yet had the soft, longer coat more characteristic of the Yorkshire Terrier. These puppies were the blueprint for today's Silky Terrier.

By the early 1900s, the Silky Terrier had a dedicated following in Australia.

What's in a Name?

A dedicated following to these unique puppies began to emerge in several states within Australia. By the early 1900s, dog organizations in at least two of these states had established individual breed standards for their Silky Terriers. The breed was named the Sydney Silky Terrier in one state, and the Victorian Silky Terrier in another. By establishing a breed standard, the kennel club in each state created a workable plan to further help establish the Silky Terrier as an individual breed, and began to promote those Silky Terriers already in existence.

The formation of the Australian National Kennel Council in 1959 helped to unify the breed within the country. One standard was adopted to be used throughout the country, and the name Australian Silky Terrier was officially adopted.

Silky Terrier, Australian Terrier, or Yorkshire Terrier?

The Silky Terrier is a breed that might be considered a relative newcomer to the dog world. Interbreeding in Australia was commonly allowed until the early 1930s, so the three breeds used in the creation of the Silky Terrier have many similarities. Subtle differences among the breeds do exist, and can be used to correctly identify the breed in question.

The Yorkshire Terrier, Silky Terrier, and Australian Terrier are related, but have subtle differences in size, coat, and attitude.

Size Considerations

The Australian Terrier is the largest of the three breeds, averaging 10 to 11 inches when measured at the withers. The Silky Terrier is slightly smaller in size, with an average height of 9 to 10 inches, and is more moderate in weight. The Yorkshire Terrier is considerably smaller than its "cousins," and has a lighter body frame. When looking at the Silky Terrier from the side, the body will appear just slightly longer than its own height. In contrast, the Australian Terrier is longer backed in proportion to its height, while the Yorkshire Terrier should have a short back, creating a somewhat square appearance.

Show Dogs

The first Silky Terrier to be exhibited at a dog show in Australia was known as Ideal, shown in 1905 and 1906 at the Sydney Royal Dog Show in the "Terrier, Soft and Silky" class. Ideal's sire was Sandow—an Australian Terrier.

The head of the Silky Terrier and the Australian Terrier remain quite similar to this day. The one noticeable difference is the topknot, or hair over the forehead between the ears. In the Silky Terrier this is more profuse, while in the Australian Terrier the topknot is less elegant, only covering the top of the skull. The Australian Terrier also does not have a part down the middle of its head, one of the characteristic trademarks of the Silky Terrier. The Yorkshire Terrier's

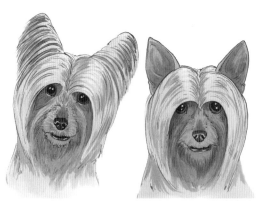

When properly groomed, the Silky Terrier's head has a clean muzzle and ears, and the characteristic center part.

head reflects its "toy size" and is quite noticeably smaller than either the Silky Terrier or Australian Terrier, with abundant hair fringes. The topknot of the Yorkshire Terrier is very long and elaborate, and is often pulled up and secured with a bow to accentuate the pretty face.

Coat of Many Colors

Not surprisingly, the most noticeable trait that separates the Silky Terrier from both the Yorkshire Terrier and the Australian Terrier is its coat. While the fine, silky texture is very similar in both the Silky Terrier and Yorkshire Terrier, the coat of the Silky Terrier should not be so long or profuse that it touches the floor, as is common in the Yorkshire Terrier. The Australian Terrier has a double coat consisting of a softer undercoat, protected by a harsh outercoat, while the Silky Terrier carries a single coat of soft, fine hair.

Even the blue and tan color that originally helped to create the Silky Terrier has subtle differences among the three breeds. The adult Yorkshire Terrier has a dark, steel-blue coat color. The blue body coat in the adult Australian Terrier can range in intensity from a dark, steel blue to a silver blue. The Silky Terrier's blue color is considerably lighter, commonly a silver blue or slate blue.

The tan color on the head of the Silky Terrier should be a deep, rich color. The tan fades to a less intense fawn or silver color on the topknot. By contrast, the tan coloration of the Yorkshire Terrier's head has no fading; instead, it deepens along the sides of the head. It is interesting to note that puppies of all three breeds are born with a darker body coat color. Some puppies are so dark that the coat is black, fading to the color that is specified by its breed's unique genetic code.

The coat of a Silky Terrier should not be so long that it touches the floor.

Small Dogs, Big Attitudes

The Silky Terrier also has a different attitude from its Australian Terrier and Yorkshire Terrier relatives. One of the traits that makes the Silky Terrier so appealing is that, in spite of its smaller size, the Silky Terrier has a bit of a "Napoleon complex," often taking on the bold attitude of a much larger dog. The Silky Terrier lacks some of the natural aggressiveness that can be commonly found in the Australian Terrier, while displaying none of the shyness or nervousness that may be commonly associated with the Yorkshire Terrier.

The Silky Terrier today retains some of the qualities of both the Australian Terrier and Yorkshire Terrier, yet remains a breed that is uniquely rugged and playful.

The Silky Terrier's American Debut

The Silky Terrier first appeared in the United States in the 1930s. The public got its first look at this adorable breed when a pair of Silkies,

Cover Boy
A Silky Terrier puppy, Redway Blue Boy, graced the cover of *This Week* magazine on November 28, 1954.

called Sydney Silky Terriers at the time, were featured in an issue of *National Geographic* in 1936. By the next decade, the Silky had begun to be imported at a steady rate, with dog lovers from coast to coast promoting the breed.

The decade spanning the 1950s might be the time frame most responsible for the Silky's popularity in the United States. The growth of the breed at this time was at a frenzied pace, with photographs featuring Silky Terrier puppies and articles capturing the spunky personality appearing in print from *Sports Illustrated* to *This Week* magazine.

The scruffy, impish look of the Silky puppy appealed to many, from average families to famous movie stars. It is estimated that during this decade the breed's popularity rose from less than 50 in the early 1950s to approximately 600 in the late 1950s. It was also during this decade that the breed's name was changed as well, from the Sydney Silky Terrier to the Australian Silky Terrier. Another name change followed when, with its acceptance into the toy group in 1959, the Silky Terrier became the 113th recognized American Kennel Club (AKC) breed.

The Silky Terrier Today

Today, the Silky Terrier enjoys a popularity that remains steady and unchanging among its many admirers. The Silky Terrier ranked 65th

The Silky Terrier is neat in appearance, but does not appear to be sculpted or scissored.

among all AKC breeds in 2005, and is the 14th most common toy breed registered with the American Kennel Club. As our society continues to grow, and space becomes more limited, the Silky Terrier is poised to fit perfectly into many modern family households.

The Silky Terrier Standard

The breed standard is a written guideline used to create a mental picture of the "perfect" Silky Terrier. Each individual part of a Silky Terrier is mentioned, providing a blueprint for perfection. Highlights of the current breed standard include:

General Appearance: The Silky Terrier is a true "toy terrier." The body is slightly longer than tall, of refined bone structure, but of sufficient substance to suggest the ability to hunt and kill domestic rodents. The coat is silky in texture, parted from the stop to the tail and presents a well groomed but not sculpted appearance. An inquisitive nature and joy of life make this breed an ideal companion.

Size: Shoulder height from 9 to 10 inches. The body is about one-fifth longer than the dog's height.

Substance: Lightly built with strong but rather fine bone.

Head: The head is wedge-shaped and moderately long. The expression is piercingly keen, the eyes small, dark, and almond shaped. Ears are small, V-shaped, set high, and carried erect. The skull is slightly longer than the muzzle. The nose is black. Teeth are strong and well aligned in scissors bite.

Neck, Topline, and Tail: The neck fits gracefully into sloping shoulders. The topline is level. The tail is docked, set high, and carried at 12 to 2 o'clock position.

Forequarters: Forelegs are strong, straight, and rather fine-boned. Feet are small, catlike, round, and compact. Nails are strong and dark colored. The feet point straight ahead. Dewclaws, if any, are removed.

Hindquarters: Thighs are well muscled and strong. Well angulated stifles are parallel when viewed from behind.

Your Silky's tail will need to be trimmed to create a well coated, but neat appearance.

Coat: Straight, single, glossy, silky in texture. On adults, the coat falls below and follows the body outline. It should not approach floor length. On the top of the head, the hair is so profuse as to form a topknot. Hair on the face and ears should not be long. The hair is parted on the head and down over the back. The tail is well coated but devoid of plume.

Color: Either blue and tan. The blue may be silver blue, pigeon blue, or slate blue, the tan deep and rich. The blue extends from the base of the skull to the tip of the tail, down the forelegs to the elbows, and halfway down the outside of the thighs. The blue should be very dark on the tail. Tan appears on muzzle and cheeks, around the base of the ears, on the legs and feet, and around the vent. The topknot should be silver or fawn, which is lighter than the tan points.

Gait: Should be free and lively.

Temperament: The keenly alert air of the terrier is characteristic, without shyness or excessive nervousness. The manner is quick, friendly, and responsive.

The complete breed standard can be found on the web sites for the Silky Terrier Club of America and the American Kennel Club.

On the lookout for fun!

LIVING THE GOOD LIFE

Life with a Silky Terrier is never dull. A true terrier at heart, he will not allow you to forget that he is a member of your family.

So what is it about this unique toy dog that endears it to its loyal fans? Is it the Silky Terrier's compact size, or perhaps the "confident attitude"? Ask any Silky Terrier owner or breeder, and they will tell you that it is the strong devotion that their Silky has to its owner and family that has them hooked on forever owning a Silky Terrier.

As you begin your journey into being "owned by a Silky," you will need to have an understanding of what motivates your Silky. Success in molding your Silky into a great companion mandates that you set house rules and have the ability to make sure that he follows them. Motivating a Silky Terrier to follow your rules can be a challenging task, one that can be achieved with a constant mixture of appropriately timed rewards and firm disci-

The Silky Terrier enjoys each moment he spends with his family.

pline. If you fail to recognize your Silky's personality, his determination, combined with his need to be involved in your daily activities, will be a constant reminder!

The Silky Terrier Temperament

The Silky Terrier is sometimes referred to as a "one family" breed, as many adult Silkys can appear somewhat aloof with strangers. The Silky Terrier's affection for his owner is very strong, so your Silky may see very little need to promote his good qualities to every new person he meets. The Silky Terrier holds a strong devotion to his family and friends. At times, he seems almost human, gazing inquisitively as he tries to understand every word that is being said. He enjoys every ounce of affection he receives, soaking up each stroke of the hand, often with his eyes closed in a moment of

══ T I P ══

Take a Leading Role

Leadership from a Silky's perspective is complex. You can establish a leadership role by remembering a few simple things:

Leaders are confident. Giving commands in an upright, standing position signals a leadership posture.

Leaders speak and others listen. Your vocal tones should convey that you are in charge. Commands should be in a deep tone of voice and given with an authoritative tone, and you should not have to yell. Praise should be given in an upbeat, happy tone of voice.

Lead by example. Your body language and your voice must reflect the same goal.

In order for your Silky Terrier to live up to your expectations, certain rules must be established, and every member of your household must be "on board," allowing no "cheating." This leads to a well-adjusted, calm Silky Terrier.

Some examples of household rules are:

1. Is your Silky allowed on furniture or beds?

2. Is it OK to feed your Silky foods other than dog treats or kibble?

3. Where will your Silky sleep?

4. Where will your Silky eat?

relaxation. The Silky Terrier truly cherishes the time he spends with his family. He looks forward to those quiet evenings watching television, relaxed walks together, and quiet naps. He freely offers affectionate kisses to those near and dear to him, wanting nothing but a kind word or a quick pat on the head in return.

It is also important to remember that many Silky Terriers are aware of their surroundings at all times, often ready for action at the slightest sound or motion. Your Silky may be moderate in size, but he is big in attitude! At times, he may prefer to sit next to you instead of on your lap, perhaps instinctively on the alert, in true terrier fashion. The Silky Terrier can be an independent breed, but his personality blossoms in a family that offers the right combination of love and affection.

The adolescent or young Silky Terrier can be energetic, even a bit trying at times. His strong willed, inquisitive nature demands that you, his owner, be equally as determined at succeeding in teaching him to abide by your house rules and the importance of good manners. Silky Terriers are smart, eager to learn, and willing to please, but they can be somewhat challenging to motivate!

The Importance of Leadership

No matter what your Silky Terrier's age may be, it is vital that he regard you as a leader. Your Silky wants to be an integral member of your family, and in the absence of a clear leader, he may try to become one himself.

It is especially important that every member of your family knows that there are "house rules" when talking about your Silky's behavior, and that those rules are to be consistently followed and applied to your Silky Terrier's day-to-day routine. It can be difficult to change a Silky Terrier's mind once it is set, so why not start out by clearly defining what you will allow and what you consider clearly unacceptable behavior?

Silky Terrier puppies are hard to resist!

Those Silky Terriers who unfortunately find themselves in rescue programs, humane societies, or shelters are often relinquished for behaviors that may have been easier to control or completely eliminated had their owners clearly demonstrated that they were in charge on a consistent basis.

The Importance of Socialization

If your Silky Terrier is less than six months of age, he is no doubt the center of attention whenever he appears in public. A Silky puppy is a bit of a novelty and irresistible to be around. This is the perfect age to teach your Silky that, while he may not have to show outward affection toward strangers, he is expected to tolerate their presence. Remember, the adult Silky Ter-

rier is very loyal to his owner, and although his temperament is generally outgoing, he may see no real reason to interact affectionately with those he does not know. If he has not been properly socialized, this indifference may turn into intolerance and, in some cases, an outward display in defense of his "person."

One of the best ways to socialize the young Silky Terrier is to positively expose him to different people in controlled situations. Short trips to the veterinary clinic, groomer, or children's functions should be made into a learning experience for your Silky Terrier. A great way to change your Silky's mind about strangers is to make a tasty treat available to him from each new person he meets. If every "outsider" becomes a source of something yummy, it does not take long before your Silky learns not only to accept each new person he encounters, but to look forward to each new interaction.

The adult Silky might require a bit more persuasion to change his mind about people. The "meet new person, get food treat" method may work a bit more slowly, or may not seem to make much of a difference. If he doesn't seem at all moved by a food treat, you might want to try having new people toss a favorite toy his way.

Socialization of the adult Silky Terrier should not be forced; if your Silky becomes nervous, anxious, or fearful, then the routine is counterproductive, and forcing him to accept a stranger could do more harm than good.

Socialization of the young Silky Terrier should also include positive encounters with other dogs, both large and small. Adult Silky Terriers often forget their small stature, and when encountering another dog, can become very vocal and defensive. This overzealous behavior can be minimized with early socialization encounters that allow your young Silky Terrier to learn that "play dates" with other dogs are fun!

Many training facilities, boarding kennels, or grooming shops now offer "day care" options. When managed correctly, supervised play sessions between dogs of similar size, age, and temperament can be a valuable long-term tool in teaching proper social dog behavior. The young or adolescent Silky Terrier that plays with others gains not only the knowledge of proper play behaviors, but is given a wonderful outlet for all that bouncy terrier energy!

Even adult Silky Terriers can enjoy supervised encounters with other dogs, although most are intent on controlling the playtime instead of participating in it.

Silkys and Children

Children and dogs have been a wonderful combination in many stories. What is cuter than a child and a puppy, playing together or taking a walk through the neighborhood? Adding a dog to the family is often the next step to completing the perfect family portrait, and the Silky Terrier can be a wonderful addition to many families if there is a good understanding of the terrier temperament and its potential difficulties.

The Silky Terrier can be a great addition to the right family.

The Silky Terrier can be a challenge to own all by himself, without the distractions of raising children added to the picture. His curiosity may lead to trouble with the toys and clothing of small children. Silky Terriers instinctively enjoy a game of "grab it and shake it," and this behavior may lead to problems if he decides that children's clothing makes an excellent tug toy. The terrier instinct can also be a problem in families that include toddlers, as Silkys have a great ability to find food in those little hands. Jumping on toddlers and grabbing food from them, inadvertently knocking them over in the process, is a potential issue you may face if your family has small children.

Many Silky Terriers will also instinctively protect their home and their people. If your children have friends coming over with great frequency, your Silky may bark to alert you that there are other children present. Some Silky Terriers may even try to control those children by nipping, especially if a child's behavior is out of control. Silky Terriers like order and routine in their household, and they feel that there is no harm in letting rambunctious children know that they are in charge.

Families that have adolescent children are often the perfect fit for a Silky Terrier. If your family life is quiet, orderly, and manageable, a Silky Terrier can give you the satisfaction of having a small dog that the kids won't consider a "sissy." The Silky Terrier is a breed that does not shed, so it can be considered as a choice for those families whose children have allergies.

No, No—Bad Silky!

The strong terrier background and the often stubborn, independent personality of the Silky

TIP

Quiet Time

To correct obsessive barking, the first objective is to interrupt the barking sequence. There are many tools you can use—a squirt bottle of water, "shaker can," or remote bark collars are all effective barking deterrents. The correction should be timed during the actual barking behavior, and verbal praise should be immediately given as soon as the barking stops and your Silky is quiet.

can prove very challenging for the novice Silky Terrier owner. It takes a firm hand, rules that are unbending, and a good deal of patience to raise a well-behaved Silky.

Do not let the Silky's "toy" status fool you. This little dog demands to be treated as if he were a big dog. Failure to set limits will result in an out of control, bossy Silky.

Some of the more common "bad behaviors" that Silky Terriers can exhibit are preventable if dealt with immediately when the behavior surfaces, and you know what to be prepared for.

Barking Behaviors

Inappropriate barking could be considered the most common bad behavior that the Silky Terrier exhibits, and yet this problem can be quickly curbed if it is corrected early. Repetitive, out of control barking is all too often aimed at passersby walking outside your window, birds or other animals invading your Silky's yard, or cars driving down the street.

It is important to remember that the Silky patrols his territory, and his natural hunting instinct for small rodents puts him on the alert at all times. Barking is your Silky's way of communicating to everyone within earshot that he is there and that he is ready to take charge of any situation that happens to come his way.

Digging

The Silky Terrier's strong desire to rid his property of rodents is one of the driving forces behind uncontrolled digging behaviors. Small movements along the ground, as innocent as leaves blowing in the wind, can throw your Silky's digging

instinct into high gear. Another explanation for digging is boredom if your Silky Terrier is left outside for too long a period of time.

To eliminate the damage from digging, do not leave your Silky outside without supervision for long periods of time, and be sure to provide another activity to hold his attention while he is enjoying the great outdoors.

Aggression

Aggression is one of the most serious behavioral issues that the owner of an out of control Silky may face. His inborn need to manage his environment can predispose your Silky to outbursts in attitude if you are unable to assume and maintain the leadership role.

Aggression can be defined as a threatening gesture by your Silky Terrier toward a person or persons, or another dog. Aggressive gestures might include barking in an outwardly threatening manner, snarling or baring teeth, growling, snapping or attempting to bite.

Dogs who repeatedly threaten others are difficult to live with, and this behavior should not be taken lightly. You should not make excuses for the inappropriate behavior, as an "ostrich approach" will most certainly lead to more trouble in the future. Each encounter your Silky sees as a successful defense of his "space" gives him added confidence and validates his behavior.

The aggressive Silky Terrier should be dealt with quickly, before his reactions become habitual. A veterinary behavioral therapist or a professional trainer should be consulted for any aggressive event, and a program for decreasing the behavior should be formulated before his behavior becomes intolerable.

Even at rest, your Silky will always be ready for action.

SOLD ON SILKYS

You are captivated by this inquisitive, bold little breed. It is time now to make a decision about where to get your Silky. Then you'll begin the fun, yet at times challenging task of "bringing up baby."

Once you have decided that a Silky Terrier will make the perfect addition to your family, you must begin to search for that special puppy. Where will you find that puppy that seems to be the "right one"? The source you choose your Silky Terrier from is perhaps the most important decision you have to make. How your Silky Terrier is raised before you bring her home directly affects how well she will adjust to her new home and your family. The experiences she has at an early age will play a part in how well behaved she is in the future as an adult.

All Breeders Are Not Created Equal

For most prospective Silky Terrier owners, the search for a puppy begins by locating a breeder. Deciding on which breeder may be the

Finding the right puppy for your family takes time and patience.

best means doing your homework. Dog breeders are not universally licensed, and most states do not regulate or inspect breeders on any regular basis. It is up to you to ask the right questions regarding breeding practices, care of the puppies, and any potential health problems before you consider the purchase of a Silky puppy. Do not be surprised or offended if a breeder asks questions about you as well!

The Educated Breeder

The Silky Terrier is not always an easy dog to understand, train, or breed. The educated breeder has spent many years learning how to live with her Silky Terriers and has given countless hours of love, patience, and guidance to her own Silkys before delving into the world of breeding.

Educated breeders are most often involved in showing their Silkys competing at dog shows in an effort to help evaluate those dogs that they intend to use for breeding. Once a litter of Silky puppies arrives, the educated breeder observes

Still the Same Puppy

Surgically altering your Silky Terrier will not negatively change your Silky's behavior. Female Silkys are "spayed," while male Silkys are "neutered."

each puppy's behavior and can place the puppy with the right temperament in your loving home. Silky puppies from educated breeders are often sold to pet homes on a "limited registration" basis, with the sole intention of seeing those puppies loved in their new homes as pampered pets. Once your Silky has become an adult, she can become somewhat demanding of

your time, so the educated breeder requires that your new puppy be spayed or neutered. The educated breeder understands that surgically altered Silkys make terrific pets, and will do her best to help you learn the behavioral and health benefits that are associated with neutering your new Silky puppy.

Finding that educated breeder can be a bit of a task, as breeders seldom need to do any advertising to sell their puppies. One of the best sources for locating an educated breeder is the Silky Terrier Club of America. Their web site, *www.SilkyTerrierClubofAmerica.org,* can link you to breeders committed to improving the Silky Terrier breed by practicing responsible breeding practices.

An educated Silky Terrier breeder is just as concerned about what type of Silky Terrier owner you will be. As you communicate with these breeders, they will be asking you questions regarding your knowledge of the breed, your home and family, as well as how much time you intend to devote to your Silky Terrier. After all, this breed cannot be ignored, and it is important that you understand that you must commit the time and effort to care for and train your new Silky. Do not be offended or upset if it feels like you are under the breeder's microscope. The more information an educated breeder has about you and your family, the easier it is to decide which puppy has the personality that will best fit into your family.

One of the most frustrating situations for you may be the wait for a Silky Terrier puppy. Once you have decided that this is the breed

To avoid any misunderstanding, make sure you read and understand the contract before you buy a puppy.

for you, it may be difficult to be patient about waiting for the right puppy. Educated breeders do not typically breed often, and it can be disappointing for you to hear that you will have to wait for a puppy. One important fact to remember is that many adult behavioral issues can be minimized or prevented if your Silky puppy is socialized properly at a very early age by its breeder. As difficult as it can be, waiting for the right puppy from an educated breeder can be one of the best decisions you make for your new Silky's future.

The Hobby Breeder

The hobby breeder typically produces Silky Terrier puppies specifically for sale to the pet buyer. A hobby breeder often produces three or more litters per year in his home. It is not uncommon for the hobby breeder to have one male Silky and several female Silkys that are used to produce puppies.

The hobby breeder enjoys living with Silky Terriers, but may not devote much time to honestly evaluating the dogs that he uses to breed. The hobby breeder may not know what health issues the grandparents or great-grandparents have faced, which could become a problem for you if you purchase a Silky puppy and later find there is a health issue.

While hobby breeders may provide a more readily available source for you to purchase a Silky puppy, ask for references of individuals who have previously purchased a puppy. Taking the time to check with those references should be considered a mandatory step if you intend to purchase a puppy. If you should encounter a problem once your new puppy is home, be it behavioral or medical, you want to be certain that your puppy's breeder will be there to help

Pet quality or show prospect—which one is for you?

you answer any questions and solve the problem in a timely manner.

The hobby breeder may advertise his puppies either in newspaper ads, magazines, or for sale through Internet sites.

Commercial Breeders

Commercial breeders produce large numbers of puppies exclusively for the pet market. A commercial breeder typically breeds many different types of dogs, and may keep breeding stock in conditions that are less than suitable for ensuring excellent mental and physical health for both the parents and the puppies they produce.

The commercial breeder rarely spends much time enjoying the company of canine companionship, and cannot begin to appreciate the antics of the Silky Terrier! Puppies produced by the commercial breeder are strictly a source of

TIP

Questions for Breeders

Here are some questions you should ask every breeder before you buy a Silky Terrier puppy:

✔ How long have you owned Silkys?
✔ How many Silkys do you have?
✔ How many litters of Silkys have you bred?
✔ How many litters do you produce each year?
✔ What short-term and long-term health guarantees do you offer?
✔ What health problems might I encounter if I buy one of your pups?
✔ Can I visit the mother and/or father?
✔ At what age may we visit the litter?
✔ Are you a member of any kennel club? Do you show your Silkys?
✔ May I have references of previous puppy buyers? May I contact them?
✔ Are your Silky Terriers registered with the American Kennel Club?

income, and are commonly sold to dog brokers for resale to you. Typically, commercial breeders rarely screen for health problems and have very little knowledge regarding any health issues that may be lurking in your puppy's past.

In Breeder, We Trust

There are several crucial factors you must consider when making the final decision on whom to trust regarding your Silky Terrier purchase. First, you need to ask at what age the breeder will allow your Silky puppy to join your family. Eight weeks of age is the minimum age that your Silky's breeder should consider separating her from her littermates. All puppies between six and eight weeks of age are enjoying a critical social development period and must interact with each other in order to learn proper social skills. These skills are the same ones your new Silky needs to be prepared to fit into your family, so she should not be short-changed by leaving her siblings too early.

It is not uncommon for some breeders to want to keep puppies until ten to twelve weeks of age before letting them join their new families. Educated breeders often wait to evaluate which puppies have the best show potential and may keep their puppies long enough to be certain that they are placing the right puppy in your home. Be patient, and don't push to bring home your new baby. You must trust your breeder enough to make the right decisions at this important time.

Another factor to consider when making the decision to purchase a Silky puppy is the contract your breeder offers at the time of sale. A properly written contract should include several key pieces of information about your puppy. The puppy's registration number, date of birth, sex, and color should be clearly available, as well as the name and registration numbers of both her sire and dam.

Make sure that you read the contract and are able to understand what you are expected to do as the new owner BEFORE you sign it. Are there nutritional or medical restrictions you must follow? The contract should outline any special instructions that the breeder expects you to follow, and you must be comfortable with those instructions as they are outlined, or your contract may not remain valid.

The breeder's future responsibilities should also be clearly defined in the contract. You are making a commitment to a new puppy, so ideally you are looking for a breeder who offers a short-term health guarantee, as well as a long-term guarantee defining the breeder's intentions if your Silky should encounter any serious or debilitating health problems in the future. The contract should clearly state whether the breeder intends to provide you with any monetary compensation for major health issues, and what you must do in order to fulfill the compensation request. Perhaps that most important "pitfall" in health guarantees is whether you will need to return your Silky to the breeder in order to receive compensation. Many breeders will not provide reimbursement for out-of-pocket expenses, but will instead offer to give you a replacement puppy.

An important piece of information you will want before you bring home a Silky puppy is the vaccination status of your puppy. You should inquire as to what vaccines your new puppy will have before you make the journey home. A properly vaccinated puppy is able to handle the stress of moving into a new environment more easily, and is less susceptible to illness in the first few weeks of her new home. One word of caution regarding your Silky puppy's vaccinations—MORE IS NOT BETTER. Vaccinations given before six weeks of age may be overcome by the natural immunity from the mother, rendering them ineffective. It is recommended that vaccinations be given two to three weeks apart; too many vaccines given at an early age may actually have negative effects on your puppy's immune system as she matures.

Finally, cost may be a factor in the decision of where to purchase your Silky Terrier. The cost

Both boys and girls make excellent pets.

of a Silky puppy may vary from one area of the country to another. Factors such as show quality or pet quality, registration status, availability, or the amount of health care given by the breeder can affect the cost you can expect to pay for a Silky Terrier. There is no monetary measure, however, for the knowledge and advice you will receive from sources such as the educated breeder. Remember that a less expensive puppy does not always equate to savings. A carefully bred, well-socialized Silky Terrier puppy may cost a bit more to bring home, but over the next ten to twelve years, the savings of living with a happy, healthy Silky cannot be measured in dollars and cents.

Pink or Blue?

It is also worth mentioning that the sex of a Silky puppy may be a factor in whether or not it is the perfect puppy for you. Both male and

Do Your Homework

When searching for a Silky puppy, here are some potential pitfalls to avoid:

✔ If your search for a puppy brings you to the local newspaper, check the phone numbers carefully.

If the same phone number appears several times, offering puppies for sale of different breeds, the puppies are being sold by a puppy broker or dog dealer. Brokers purchase puppies from commercial breeders at low prices and resell them at a profit. They will often tell prospective buyers that the litter was bred by a friend or relative out of state, and they are helping to sell the puppies.

✔ If you search for a puppy on the Internet, be cautious with out-of-state breeders who offer to ship your puppy.

A beautiful web site does not mean that they are a reputable source for a puppy. Check references carefully and, if it is at all possible, drive or fly to pick up your puppy and visit the breeder's home. If the breeder refuses to allow you to come pick up the puppy, or offers to meet you halfway because he has other puppies to sell in your area, this could also mean that the breeder is really a commercial breeder. Hobby breeders with poor living conditions will also refuse to allow you to visit.

✔ As you search for a puppy, you may visit potential breeders.

If a breeder has more than two breeds that she is actively breeding, she might be considered a commercial breeder as well. In some areas, the adults may be kept in a barn or garage, and only the puppies are located in the breeder's home. Socialization is key with the Silky Terrier, so purchasing a puppy from this situation may result in temperament issues later.

✔ You should be clear about the type of registration papers that your Silky Puppy will have.

The American Kennel Club (AKC) is considered the "gold standard" of registration. AKC registered puppies have a pedigree that can be accurately traced and documented. You should be aware that some hobby breeders and commercial breeders do not register with the AKC in an effort to avoid inspection. You may be offered a puppy that is registered with one of the following organizations:

American Pet Registry (APR)
Continental Kennel Club (CKC)
American Dog Breeders Association (ADBA)
World Wide Kennel Club (WWKC)

It is important to understand that a Silky Terrier puppy that is registered with one of the other organizations is NOT the same and is not transferable to an AKC registration.

female Silkys can make excellent additions to any family.

Many prospective Silky owners are afraid to purchase a male puppy, as they have been misinformed about "wandering" and "leg lifting" or "marking" tendencies in male dogs. The truth is that if your male Silky puppy is neutered at an early age, properly housebroken and trained, these "boy dog problems" should be nonexistent. Many Silky Terrier breeders and owners actually describe their male Silkys as more affectionate than their female counterparts.

Female Silky Terriers can also exhibit marking behavior if they are not spayed. Any Silky Terrier may not remain a "homebody" when unsupervised or improperly confined while outside, leaving you to ponder the question "Why is the grass greener at your neighbor's home?"

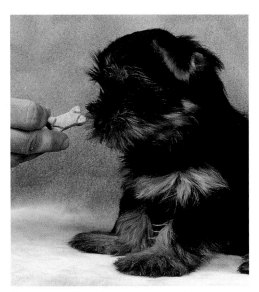

Separation from littermates is a big adjustment, so he may not eat well in the beginning.

The Search Is Over

You have researched your breeder, and she has become equally comfortable with you and your family. The wait for your puppy is finally over, and you are about to bring home your new Silky baby. The first few days are a period of many adjustments and challenges for both you and your Silky puppy. It is now up to you to make this transition as easy as possible for your new family member.

Bringing Home Baby

The first 24 to 48 hours can be quite traumatic from your new puppy's perspective. Imagine leaving all that you have known, your family and your home, and then having to start all over in a new country with people who are completely unfamiliar and do not speak your language! As difficult as it might be, it is a good idea to keep visitors to a minimum to give your new puppy time to adjust to her new surrounding and family. In spite of the Silky's normally bold personality, your new puppy may experience periods of shyness or confusion, whimpering and crying as she searches for her littermates in this unfamiliar environment. It is OK to talk to her in a soothing voice, to help her learn that she can count on you to keep her comfortable. A stuffed toy that is approximately the same size as your puppy can make a great substitute littermate for those first few days. It is not unusual for your new Silky puppy to have a decrease in appetite at this time. While she should still show some interest in each meal, she may eat less than your breeder recommended when you picked her up. Appetite decreases during periods of stress,

Essential Supplies

Here are a few things you will need before you bring home your new puppy:

✔ **A kennel or crate** (properly sized to fit your new puppy)

✔ **Soft blankets or crate pads** (washable)

✔ **A stuffed toy** (a pretend littermate)

✔ **Puppy food** (find out what the breeder has been feeding)

✔ **Food and water bowls**

✔ **Toys**

competition for food from her littermates has disappeared, and her activity level may be slightly decreased in her new home. After a couple of days of adjusting to the new routine, her true terrier playfulness will resume, and with that, a resurgence in appetite.

If, after a couple of days, her appetite does not return to what your breeder indicated was normal, a call to your veterinarian is recommended.

Housebreaking Your Silky

Your Silky puppy has a tough time ahead of her, trying to learn a very new and different routine in your home. While the Silky Terrier is still considered a toy breed, she is anything but fragile. The Silky's trainability is more like a terrier—smart and quick to learn, making housebreaking an easier task for both of you.

In the Beginning

Before you begin housebreaking, let's dispel a very common myth about the definition of "housebroken." Many new Silky owners have a predetermined age or time frame in which they believe that their puppy should be housebroken. The "magic number" often centers around one year of age. The truth is that your Silky should be considered housebroken ONLY AFTER she has had no accidents for 8 to 12 weeks. Considering the many factors that affect housebreaking—your puppy's physical development, feeding schedules, the amount of supervision she receives, and access to the right potty area, to name a few—your puppy's success depends largely on you!

If you fail to properly supervise your puppy, you will have accidents to clean up!

The Golden Rule

Housebreaking is an easy task if you know the golden rule—housebreaking your Silky is 90 percent owner perseverance and 10 percent Silky puppy development. In order for your puppy to be successful, you must be committed to having a Silky that will be accident free in the future. Housebreaking will progress quickly if you can remember these two words: **confinement** and **supervision**.

Potty Time

Before you begin housebreaking your Silky, you need to decide where you want your puppy to go to the bathroom. This "potty spot" can be located indoors by using newspaper or potty pads, or outside in an area you designate. In order to make this process easy for your new puppy, you should choose only one location. Giving your puppy the option of both an "indoor spot" as well as an "outdoor spot" can cause confusion and slow down your puppy's progress.

Once you have picked out the "spot," begin to take your Silky there frequently. Place your puppy on the spot and use a key phrase such

Potty pads can aid in housebreaking your Silky Terrier.

as "*Go potty*" to stimulate your puppy. Raising your voice to a high pitch signals excitement, so do not be afraid to sound a bit silly the first few days. This is a time for your puppy to get down to business, so do not play with her. You can walk a few steps to keep your puppy moving, which also helps stimulate the puppy to eliminate. When your puppy eliminates, praise her quietly with "*Good potty*" and pet her once she has finished, or give her a small treat. The more frequently you take your Silky to the potty area and she is successful, the quicker she will get the idea of housebreaking. Your Silky puppy will appreciate your excitement at a job well done!

If you fail to properly supervise your puppy, you will find "mistakes." Accidents will occur, especially in the first few weeks. Your Silky

The more frequently you take your Silky puppy outside, the more quickly she will become housebroken.

involved in when you grabbed her and whisked her away to be "punished." Remember that if your Silky puppy had the opportunity to make a "mistake," it means that she was not confined and was left unsupervised for a period of time. What was the Golden Rule? Silky Terriers that become housebroken quickly had owners who confined their puppies appropriately, and supervised them at all times!

What about your Silky's potty needs overnight? In general, if your Silky is less than 12 weeks of age, her physical capability to remain clean and dry (if properly confined) is no longer than four hours. This means that for the first few weeks after you bring her home, you will need to get up and take your Silky to the potty spot in the middle of the night to urinate. If getting up to take your puppy outside is not an option, you will need to give your puppy an alternative overnight area to sleep, where cleaning up mistakes is not a problem.

As your Silky puppy matures, her muscle tone improves and her ability to remain clean overnight should increase. As she gets older, the need to eliminate in the middle of the night should disappear. One note of caution: allowing your puppy to eliminate at will overnight hinders your puppy's need to control her bladder and bowel tone, making housebreaking a slow and difficult process.

Overnight trips to the "spot" can also be minimized if your puppy's water access is restricted in the evening. It is a great idea to pick up your puppy's water bowl one to two hours after she eats. If you take her for a walk or play with her

puppy may take several months before she truly learns where you expect her to eliminate. If you catch your puppy in the process of an "oops," startle her by shouting or clapping your hands, pick her up and take her directly to the "spot." Once she finishes in the correct place, praise her and then return to clean up the "mistake."

If you happen to find that your Silky puppy has left you a "present," it does no good to try to punish your puppy. Showing your puppy her "mistake," rubbing her nose in it, or getting angry serves no purpose in the housebreaking process. Your Silky puppy cannot understand that you are upset by something she did minutes or hours ago; however, she does understand that you are angry by your body language and tone of voice. She will quickly learn to associate your displeasure with whatever activity she was and she becomes thirsty after her water becomes unavailable, place a small amount in the bowl and allow her to drink.

Paper Training

Silky Terriers that have an "indoor potty spot" often have a higher incidence of "mistakes." Your Silky puppy does not understand that throw rugs and other objects left lying on the floor are unacceptable indoor spots. The visual picture to her is exactly the same as newspaper or potty pads, so supervision is even more important for success!

Crate Training—The Key to a Happy Home

In the perfect world, you would have eyes in the back of your head or a camera focused on your puppy at all times to constantly supervise her. The reality is that a Silky puppy is often added to an already hectic family, and there are times when you cannot continuously supervise your puppy. Busy schedules often cannot be adjusted to meet the very real needs of a new puppy, so you must have a way to keep your inquisitive, rambunctious Silky safe from her own actions!

Crate Training Basics

An appropriately sized crate is a must for every Silky Terrier owner. The crate can aid in housebreaking, offers a safe, pleasant environment for your puppy while you are busy or away from home, and becomes your puppy's "off limits" zone if your family has children.

Your Silky's crate can easily become a favorite spot to hide her toys, the source of yummy treats, and a great place to take an afternoon nap! Think of the crate as her bedroom, somewhere you would like her to feel comfortable going to sleep. Now create a word that means "bedtime." Each time you want your puppy to go into the crate, toss a treat into the crate and say the "bedtime" word. As your Silky puppy dives into her crate for the treat, close the door and tell her what a smart puppy she is!

There are some special comforts that will make your Silky's crate the perfect place to spend time. A fleece rug or blanket that can be washed easily makes a great bed. A stuffed toy can act as a pillow and gives your Silky someone to cuddle up to while you are gone. Feeding your puppy in her crate is an excellent idea to help her feel comfortable with her new home. Another benefit of feeding her in the crate is that properly socialized puppies do not want to eliminate where they eat or sleep, aiding in the housebreaking process.

Your Silky's crate will quickly become one of her favorite spots to hang out.

Your Silky's crate is never used as a source of punishment. It is a tool, used to keep your house from becoming a big, Silky Terrier chew toy while you are gone, and to keep your Silky safe from her own curiosity when supervision from you is impossible. The smart Silky puppy owner is not afraid to use the crate at night, while she is gone for short periods of time, or during those moments when a "time out" from activity is needed. Do not be in a hurry to stop using your puppy's crate. A properly crate-trained Silky enjoys the ability to travel with her own "mobile home," and has a quiet, familiar place to hide out when family life gets hectic. Even adult Silky Terriers will return to their crates to sleep, as if enjoying a quiet reminiscence of their puppyhood.

Puppy Play Areas

What about those days when you might need to be gone for more time than you know your Silky puppy can realistically be expected to remain clean and well-behaved? For most Silky puppies, being alone for several hours is a recipe for trouble! A playpen area can be created to provide a safe, pleasant alternative to either crating your puppy too long or isolating her in an area of your home where she could easily find herself causing trouble.

Exercise pens, puppy play yards, and even children's play yards are easy to find and are a smart investment for keeping your Silky puppy safe and happy. A play area also protects your belongings and home from those sharp, destructive Silky Terrier teeth! Your puppy's crate can be easily placed inside the area, giving her a place to play and her own bed for nap time. If your Silky is not old enough to remain clean for the amount of time you will be gone, a layer of

newspaper or a puppy pad can be placed away from the crate, giving your puppy access to a place to eliminate. Don't be surprised, however, if your Silky finds this to be a nifty toy—paper can be very interesting to the young Silky puppy. Some pens can be attached to the sides of your puppy's crate, offering a more stationary area.

Don't forget, however, that the Silky Terrier is a very agile, curious breed, and your adolescent Silky may quickly learn to jump onto the top of the crate, giving her a quick escape route! Their terrier instinct may also kick in if unsupervised for a long period of time, and they may attempt to "dig" their way under the pen, leaving your floor to suffer under those strong nails.

Secondhand Silkys

Perhaps a puppy is not right for you. If you work during the day (and getting home for an afternoon break is impossible), if your schedule is busy with family activities, or if you just do not want to go through the trouble of housebreaking a Silky puppy, why not consider adopting a mature Silky Terrier through a rescue program?

Silky Terrier Rescue

Adopting an adult Silky from a rescue program or animal shelter can be a terrific way to add a Silky to your family, without some of the headaches of raising a puppy. Secondhand Silkys are looking for the right family to love them, and are often available at a reduced cost or adoption fee. The majority of them will have already been surgically altered, ready to become a new family member.

Adopting an adult Silky does have its challenges. Some Silkys are looking for a new home

If a puppy is not right for you, think about adopting a mature Silky Terrier.

simply because their previous owners became ill and could no longer care for them. Many others, however, wind up in shelters because their owners failed to be responsible and did not have enough time to train or properly care for a Silky Terrier. These Silkys are in desperate need of someone to take charge and teach them how to be well-mannered and productive canine citizens.

If you choose to look into the adoption option, it is important to keep in mind that your new Silky may have a behavioral issue that needs your attention and may require a large amount of dedication from you to change. You must look for solutions to the problem and be committed to changing the behavior; avoid becoming frustrated because your new Silky is not perfect. An adult Silky who is turned over to a rescue program or animal shelter because of behavioral problems did not get that way on her own or become out of control overnight. Her previous owner may have failed her, and it is now up to you to help her understand that there are alternative behaviors that you consider to be better!

Finding an Adult Silky

The Silky Terrier Club of America is a great source to begin looking for an adult Silky through adoption. There are members who are dedicated solely to fostering Silkys in need. An adoption application must be completed, and you may have to be interviewed prior to any placement of an adult Silky Terrier in your home.

Many animal shelters keep a breed-specific list of potential adoptive families, so you might also want to contact your local humane society or animal control facility and let them know that you are interested in adopting a Silky Terrier should one become available through their facility.

Contacting a Silky Terrier breeder can also be a good way to locate an adult Silky Terrier. Professional breeders may have a retired show dog that would be suitable for your home now that her career in the show ring is over. They may also occasionally have a young adult that looked promising as a puppy but now doesn't have what the breeder is looking for in a show dog. Most breeders also keep in contact with the owners of puppies that they have sold, and occasionally one may need to be adopted due to an upcoming move, allergies, or other circumstances that are beyond the control of the owner.

The most common behavioral complaints from the owners of young to adolescent Silky Terriers are problems that can be easily managed at a very early age.

Incomplete Housebreaking

This is the result of the Silky owner failing to properly supervise a young puppy, tolerating mistakes, and then offering the adolescent Silky too much freedom too quickly. Do's and Don'ts include:

DO supervise your Silky puppy at all times!

DO use confinement at all times when supervision is not possible.

DO offer your adolescent Silky more access to areas previously off limits one room or area at a time, adding additional areas ONLY if she has remained successful in her housebreaking for several weeks in the new area.

DON'T be in a hurry to give your Silky complete freedom to take over your home. Remember that your leadership should be an important part of your Silky's road to maturity.

Play Biting

This normal behavior for Silkys is typically exhibited by young puppies. Play biting should be corrected early, especially in households where children are part of your Silky's new family.

DO practice ZERO TOLERANCE. No Silky Terrier teeth should be allowed to contact skin, no matter how "gentle" your Silky is.

DO consider clothing an extension of your skin. Pulling on pants, robes, or sleeves should be corrected quickly.

DO use verbal correction for play biting. When your Silky puppy bites, a sharp "OW" in a loud, deep tone of voice should startle your puppy enough to trigger her to let go. Quietly praise her immediately if she backs away, and refocus her play behavior on a toy or other object.

DO use body language to convey your displeasure. When your puppy seems "out of control" with biting behaviors, stop moving, turn away from your puppy, and ignore her for ten seconds. Withdrawing from your puppy sends a strong message that you do not like her behavior.

DO intervene on the behalf of children. If they cannot give a strong enough startle sound to stop play biting, do it for them. Ask them to stand still, putting toes into the nearest wall or under a piece of furniture, and count to ten. This removes the moving target from your Silky, and the puppy will look for some activity that is more rewarding.

Use a crate to confine your Silky when supervision is impossible.

DON'T be afraid to use the crate for a "time out." If all else fails, your puppy might need a short break in her crate with a toy to keep her busy and to help her settle down.

Destructive Chewing

Chewing is a natural behavior for your Silky Terrier. Destructive chewing is the result of teething, boredom, or anxiety.

DO properly confine your Silky to eliminate access to furniture, baseboards, electrical cords, and children's belongings.

DO provide stimulating, rewarding toys for your Silky puppy to chew, play with, and rip apart. Remember that the terrier in your Silky means her play behavior may include "search and destroy."

DO look for toys that are fun and interesting. Interactive toys that feed your Silky puppy, rewarding her play behavior by dropping food rewards, are a must for every adolescent Silky Terrier.

Jumping on People

Your Silky may begin to jump on those people she knows and loves. While this behavior is tolerable as a young puppy, it soon leads to an annoying habit if it is not stopped early.

DO ignore your Silky if she begins jumping on your legs. Walk past her if she jumps on you and do not look at her. Talking to your Silky, pushing her away or picking her up encourages her to jump again.

Inappropriate chewing can be prevented by providing stimulating, rewarding chew toys for your Silky Terrier.

DO reward "four on the floor." When your Silky is either standing or sitting in front of you, pet her and praise her to reward the behavior you want.

DO use a leash to restrain your Silky when answering the door. Asking her to *"SIT"* and only opening the door when she is sitting calmly teaches her to wait patiently while visitors arrive.

DON'T pick up your Silky to answer the door. An out of control Silky who gets picked up each time she barks at the door makes your life more difficult. Use a leash for control.

DON'T allow your guests to reward bad behavior. Ask visitors not to talk to, pet, or interact with your Silky unless she is standing or sitting quietly.

SILKY SENSATIONS— GROOMING YOUR SILKY

Grooming your Silky can be quite a challenge. Your Silky may decide that this beauty routine really doesn't fit into his daily plans. With a little persistence on your part, and some quick grooming steps, your Silky will have a coat that others envy.

The Silky Terrier appeals to many owners due in part to his compact size. The soft, straight coat that has become the Silky trademark is another reason the Silky Terrier is chosen as a pet. The Silky Terrier is considered to be a non-shedding breed, and the coat is fairly easy to maintain. A small amount of shedding between puppyhood and adulthood is considered normal, as is a small amount of hair loss during the changing seasons.

The hair of the Silky Terrier is somewhat unique. The texture is more humanlike than that of most other long-coated breeds and is

Proper brushing is a necessity for keeping your Silky Terrier beautiful.

not considered "fur." The thickness and feel very closely resemble that of a human child.

Combing Out Your Silky Terrier

Proper grooming of the Silky Terrier coat requires a brushing in order to maintain its healthy shine and texture. Each Silky is slightly different, and depending on your Silky's level of activity and coat length, your brushing routine may need to be as frequently as every day, or as infrequent as once a week. A pin brush should be used to remove any tangles, dirt, or mats that may be present. The coat should be brushed in small sections, beginning with the

Silky Terrier hair has a texture similar to a human child's.

alleviate some of the discomfort that combing out tangles can cause.

Trimming the Silky Terrier Coat

The coat of the adult Silky Terrier should not be so long that it brushes the floor. The length may be trimmed occasionally, following the contour of the body, to present a clean, neat appearance. The hair on the face is generally short, and his eyebrows may be trimmed in order to allow your Silky a better view of the world. The hair between the eyes is normally trimmed into an inverted "V." While this may be more personal preference, trimming in this manner may help keep your Silky's eyes from becoming irritated by excess hair.

Grooming by a Professional

While most owners choose to own a Silky Terrier because of the trademark coat, some owners find that they cannot keep the coat correctly combed out and tangle-free. One option is to discuss "clipping" your Silky's coat with a professional dog groomer. A style similar to the clip given to the Miniature Schnauzer is most often recommended for the Silky Terrier. The body coat is clipped short, and the furnishings on the legs are either clipped or scissored to a shorter length. If your Silky Terrier's coat becomes matted, a professional grooming may be the only way to keep him comfortable.

ends of the hair. A proper brushing technique for your Silky's coat is to brush the ends first, gently working out any mats, then working back in sections toward the skin. The hair on the muzzle should be checked regularly for any food that may have accumulated. Combing out the hair on the face and head may present a special challenge, as many Silky Terriers refuse to hold still for this simple procedure. Silky Terriers often don't see a need for "being beautiful" as they are truly terriers at heart!

A "leave in" spray conditioner should always be used each time you brush your Silky's hair. This simple step keeps the hair from becoming brittle and breaking when combed, and is an aid in reducing mats and tangles. Spraying a small amount into the mat and allowing it to penetrate will also help soften the hair and

Bathing Your Silky Terrier

The Silky Terrier coat does require regular bathing to maintain its glossy shine and silky

If left untrimmed, the hair on your Silky's head will interfere with his ability to see the world around him.

texture. The adult Silky Terrier coat is beautiful to look at and a joy to the touch, so the correct choice of shampoo is an important step in the grooming routine. Silky Terriers with normal, healthy coats will benefit from a bath using a hydrating shampoo. Shampoos that have fatty acids added, are soap free, or contain oatmeal are all excellent choices for regular bathing. If the coat is exceptionally dry, with flaky skin or dandruff present, it is important to see your veterinarian before selecting a shampoo. The Silky Terrier can be prone to a variety of skin conditions, which can be controlled by regular bathing with the appropriate shampoo for the specific, diagnosed skin condition.

Occasionally, your Silky's coat may seem a bit too oily. This may be an indication of a skin problem or the result of too much coat conditioner. A shampoo that contains a "stripping agent" may

Comb your Silky's face and head following a bath to train the hair to part correctly.

be an appropriate choice. If your Silky Terrier has an oily coat, routine bathing is important, but care should be taken not to overbathe, which may then result in a dry, brittle coat.

Many Silky Terrier breeders recommend following each bath with a coat conditioner. The use of a conditioner helps to bond moisture to the hair shaft, insuring the silky coat texture and aiding in reducing mats and tangles. A conditioner may also be recommended following any medicated bath.

How your Silky Terrier is bathed can also be a factor in the overall health and appearance of his coat. Before you begin each bath, make sure to spray any tangles or mats with water or conditioner and completely brush them out. Bathing a Silky's coat when tangled will only tighten the mats, which can make further attempts at brushing an unpleasant experience. The water temperature used for bathing should be slightly warm to the touch. Bathing with water that is too hot can contribute to a dry, brittle coat.

Begin your Silky's bath by wetting down the hair on the head, neck, chest, and forelegs.

Your Silky's facial hair is generally short, and his eyebrows may be trimmed.

Continue to wet the coat on the back, sides, and underbelly, followed by the rear legs and tail. Care should be taken not to get water in the ear canals during the bathing process. A cotton ball gently placed in each ear will help prevent too much water from entering the ear. Shampoo can be applied following the same pattern as the initial wetting of the coat. A small amount of shampoo placed in your palm can be easily worked into the coat on the face and muzzle, avoiding the eyes. If you are bathing with a medicated shampoo, a drop of mineral oil can be placed into each eye to protect them from becoming irritated by the shampoo.

Work the shampoo into a lather throughout the coat, and don't forget to lather the belly, chest area, and feet. To avoid creating tangles when you work the shampoo into a lather, you should be careful not to twist or twirl your Silky's damp hair. Allow the shampoo to remain in the coat as indicated by the directions on the shampoo bottle. Once you are ready to rinse the coat, begin at the head and neck and rinse down the length of the back toward the tail. As the shampoo is rinsed out along the spine, continue to rinse it down the sides of the neck and body and off the legs and feet. Pay close attention to the underbelly and inside of the legs, as these areas can be hard to rinse and are easily missed. Repeating the rinse pattern several times will ensure that no soap remains in the coat. The Silky Terrier's coat should be completely free from shampoo before any coat conditioner is applied. Once you have a "squeaky clean" coat, the water temperature can be lowered, and a final rinse with cool water can be given to help seal in moisture and produce a healthy shine.

The Silky Terrier's coat can be allowed to air dry; however, the playful nature of the Silky almost certainly guarantees that he will find some reason to roll around on the floor before he is completely dry! Gently squeeze the water from the coat with your hands to remove any excess. The Silky's coat is easily tangled when wet, so it is advisable not to "rub" the coat with a bath towel when drying it. The proper technique is to "blot" the coat, absorbing as much of the remaining water as possible. If you choose to allow the coat to air dry, make sure that you spray it with conditioner, comb or brush out any tangles, and be prepared to keep your Silky busy with a quiet indoor activity! A handheld dryer may also be used on a cool, low setting to quickly dry the coat. Using a comb or pin brush to lift the hair in sections as you dry it will also lessen the drying time. Once your Silky's coat is completely dry, he is ready to find mischief and work on getting dirty again!

Nail Clipping

The Silky Terrier needs very little in the way of other grooming on a regular basis. Trimming your Silky's nails on a weekly or semi-weekly basis can become part of your grooming routine. If your Silky Terrier's nails are clipped on a regular basis, only the tip of each nail needs to be trimmed in order to keep the nails at a relatively short length. Many Silky Terriers are reluctant to have their feet touched or held, which may make each nail trim a test of your patience, so be prepared! If you should happen to clip the nail too short, you can use styptic powder or a styptic pencil to quickly stop the bleeding. Styptic powders are available at any pet store, and it is a good idea to have one of these products on hand before you begin each nail trim.

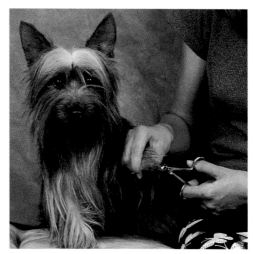

Your Silky needs to learn to accept nail trims on a regular basis.

Cleaning Your Silky Terrier's Ears

Part of the regular Silky Terrier grooming routine should also include cleaning the ears regularly. A cotton ball that is moistened with ear cleaning solution or rubbing alcohol should be used for each cleaning. To clean the ears properly, hold the tip of the ear in one hand and place the saturated cotton ball on the end of your index finger. Gently insert the cotton ball into the ear and rotate your finger, cleaning each nook and cranny. If your Silky Terrier's ears are exceptionally dirty or waxy, a small amount of cleaning solution instilled into the canal, followed by a gentle massage of the ear canal, will help loosen dirt, wax, and debris. The wax and debris are then easily removed with the cotton ball.

Placing a cotton ball in your Silky's ears before a bath helps to keep water from entering the ear.

The Silky Terrier's curious nature and love of life often result in the need for regular bathing and brushing. Fortunately, the coat of the Silky Terrier makes our job of keeping him beautiful a little bit easier, with only a little effort on the part of the owner.

If you want to keep your Silky looking his best, it is a great idea to begin a home health care routine that involves grooming and an examination. This weekly "beauty treatment" will help to insure that your Silky Terrier not only looks terrific, but feels good, too!

The following grooming routine can be quickly and easily done at home on a weekly basis:

1. Place your Silky Terrier on a table or other elevated surface. By examining your Silky in an elevated location, he is easier to work with. You can easily train your Silky Terrier to stand in place by giving him the command "*Stand*" and then rewarding him with a piece of food when all four feet are frozen in place. A suitable grooming area can be created by placing a non-slip bath mat on a counter or table top.

2. Begin to examine your Silky from head to toe. Check his eyes to make sure that they are clear and bright, and free from any discharge—and watch out for Silky Terrier kisses! Next, lift his lips to perform a dental exam. His teeth should be white and free from excessive tartar and plaque. Make sure that you check his molars at the rear of his mouth, as these tend to accumulate plaque and tartar more quickly. Any teeth that look discolored, loose, or broken, or any mouth odor, should be reported to your veterinarian.

Your Silky's ears are next. Clean each ear, using a cotton ball and ear cleaning solution. The ear should be light pink in color, and each ear canal should be easy to clean, with no swelling or redness.

Now you can use your fingers to check your Silky for tumors, especially if he is older. Your Silky will think you are giving him a massage! Move your fingers slowly over his neck, back, and sides in a small circular pattern. Check each front leg next, move on to his chest area, and then to his stomach. Finish your "massage" by checking the rear legs and his now wagging little tail!

3. Now it's time for a quick combing and check of your

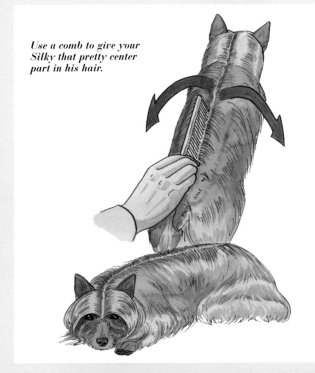

Use a comb to give your Silky that pretty center part in his hair.

Silky's skin. First, use a spray bottle to spray a section of hair with water (you can also use a spray, leave-in conditioner or a diluted cream rinse.) Comb the damp section of hair, beginning with the ends and work backwards toward the body. Take your time, working through any tangles or mats, so that you do not damage the hair. Check the skin of each section combed to make sure your Silky is free from parasites and skin disease. You can part the hair on your Silky's body using the end of the comb. Begin at the back of the ears and continue down the spine to the base of your Silky's tail. If your Silky is still a puppy, parting the hair may be difficult due to the short body coat. Part the "topknot" last, when your Silky's coat is dry. Brushing the hair on the forehead backwards, toward the ears, when damp, may help to train the hair to part naturally.

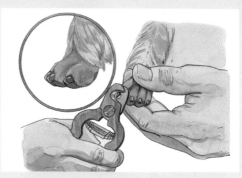

If you trim the tips of your Silky Terrier's nails each week, he'll learn to accept the routine and have short nails and beautiful feet.

4. To obtain the "clean" look on the face, ears, feet, and tail, you will need to have him professionally groomed or learn to do it yourself. Thinning shears are used to trim any long hair on the muzzle, ears, feet, and tail. Clippers are seldom necessary to trim the Silky Terrier's coat. A nice, tidy appearance to the feet can be created by using a scissors to trim the hair between the pads. Continue to scissor any long hair on the toes, following the outline of the foot.

5. The final step in your Silky's beauty treatment is a nail trim. It is best to begin this routine at an early age, as most Silky's don't believe in pedicures! Ideally, your Silky's toenails should be trimmed so that when your Silky is standing, the nails do not touch the floor. A human nail clipper can be used in young puppies, but a dog nail clipper will be needed as your Silky grows. Holding your Silky's paw in one hand, place the clipper at a slight angle on the very tip of the nail and squeeze the trimmer quickly, cutting the nail. If you clip your Silky's nails each week, you will only need to trim a small amount off each nail to keep them short. Cutting off too much of the nail, or back too close to the foot pad, will result in a cut of the "quick," or vein, in the nail. Bleeding will result, which can be controlled using a styptic powder. Your Silky will remember this "oops" next time and won't be so eager to have his nails done again!

SATISFYING YOUR SILKY

Remember the phrase "you are what you eat"? It is certainly true when it comes to balancing your Silky Terrier's diet.

Your Silky Terrier's small size means she has a unique set of nutritional requirements. Add the calories she needs to maintain her tireless energy level, and add to the equation the amino acids she will require to help keep her trademark coat in shape, and you will begin to understand that her diet plays an important role in your Silky's overall health.

Food for Thought

Ever wonder why dog food companies spend so much time and money promoting their food as the best choice for your Silky? Selling dog food is big business—it is considered to be one of the most competitive marketplaces. Many dog owners rely on those cute advertisements, the recommendations of friends and family, or

Your Silky's diet plays an important role in her overall health.

convenient options at the local supermarket as the only criteria for choosing a dog food. Your Silky Terrier is certainly not "just a dog," so her food shouldn't be "just any old food." One small step you can take to make an informed, educated decision regarding your Silky's diet is read the nutritional label on your Silky's food, and learn what the information really means. Understanding the ingredients and learning to assess the quality of the diet is not difficult, yet it has an enormous impact on your Silky's health.

Nutrient Know-how

In order to read a nutritional label, you will need to have some understanding of what the nutrients in the food are that affect your Silky, and what ingredients are best to provide those nutrients quickly and with little effort from your Silky's digestive system.

The adult Silky Terrier remains active and seems to be less prone to obesity.

Proteins

Proteins are the building blocks for your Silky Terrier. Your Silky uses proteins in her diet to form and maintain muscles, tendons, and ligaments, as well as that beautiful Silky Terrier coat and strong nails. Proteins may be one of the most important nutrients that your Silky needs, as they are converted into amino acids, and play a critical role in the development of her immune system and hormone production.

The proteins found in your Silky's diet need to be easy for her to break down and use wherever her body requires at any given moment.

This might be to help rebuild a nail broken during an excavation, to help keep muscles growing strong in a young Silky, or to replenish the immune system following stress in the older Silky. The proteins in your Silky's diet might be manufactured from either animal-based proteins, such as beef, chicken, lamb, fish, or from plant-based sources, such as soybean, wheat, or corn. The essential amino acids that your Silky needs to maintain good health are much more readily available from those foods that use animal-based sources for protein, than from those that rely on plant-based sources.

Carbohydrates

Carbohydrates are what your Silky uses to go into "overdrive," providing a tireless source of energy. Excess carbohydrates are stored in your Silky's body as fat, and may be used at a later date as energy in chasing squirrels, barking at your neighbors, or on those long, quiet walks.

Carbohydrates must be available in a usable form in order to be useful to your Silky. This form, known as soluble carbohydrates, is found in many plant proteins. Wheat and barley are two of the more common plant sources that may be found in your Silky's diet. Carbohydrates are also the main culprit in obesity in the mature Silky Terrier.

Fiber

Fiber is a nutrient that directly affects the digestibility of your Silky's diet. The fiber in your Silky's food is actually carbohydrates that are insoluble. The right amount of fiber can help your Silky absorb the other nutrients, while a diet that is too high in fiber will decrease absorption, and your Silky may not be able to meet her energy needs.

Fat

The fat content of your Silky's diet is of great importance. Fat has several purposes, all of which greatly affect your Silky's look. Fats can be utilized by your Silky as a second source of quick, reliable energy. Fat enhances absorption of the fat-soluble vitamins in the diet, notably A, D, E, and K. Fat is also broken down into fatty acids, which are required if your Silky is to display that wonderful coat. Finally, fat is used to increase or enhance palatability. If your Silky won't eat, she won't look and feel her best! Fats are found in the form of animal fats, plant oils, and fish oils.

Ingredient Information

Reading the ingredient panel on your Silky's food is like trying to understand a foreign language—you recognize certain similarities to words you know, but you aren't quite sure what they mean! The ingredients in the diet you choose to feed are important, as they are responsible for the nutrients your Silky needs.

Meat and Poultry By-products

By-products are purchased from commercial rendering plants and may include some or all of the parts of an animal. In most foods, the organs, connective tissues, bones, and blood may be included, while heads and feet may also be included in poultry by-products.

Cereal Grain Products

Grain products may include whole grain cereals such as wheat, or might be by-products produced at mills, including hulls or bran.

A quality food is easily digestible and provides the nutrition your Silky Terrier needs.

Meat and Bone Meal

Meat and bone meal is also a waste product from commercial rendering plants. It is different from meat by-products in that it is not processed with blood.

Preservatives

Most of the popular dog foods are preserved naturally, thanks to consumer awareness that came from our own eating habits. Vitamins, such as C and E, are natural preservatives and can be used successfully to keep your Silky's food fresh over a moderate length of time. Some of the cheaper foods may still be produced using artificial preservatives such as BHA, BHT, and Ethoxyquin.

Special Ingredients

The competitive dog food market has forced companies to produce diets that offer something unique or different in order to survive. Diets that contain antioxidants for joint health, additives for better dental health, diets that are "all natural" or that contain foods that might appeal to your tastes are all available.

The Puppy Palate

Silky Terrier puppies expend a lot of energy each day just trying to keep up their silly antics and mischief. In order to give your puppy the best nutrition to remain active, alert, and growing properly during her first year of age, you should look for a diet formulated for puppy growth and development. Your Silky puppy is lucky, as there are now many diets created with formulas specifically designed for small breeds (those that mature to a weight of less than 20 pounds). These diets contain higher amounts of protein and fat to meet the increased energy requirements of the active Silky Terrier puppy.

Recent research into dog nutrition has also shown the benefits of certain fatty acids to the developing brain and vision of your Silky Terrier puppy. Docosahexaenoic acid, known as DHA,

Silky Terriers, young and old, deserve the best when it comes to their diet.

has been demonstrated to increase the learning capabilities of young dogs. Puppies fed a diet that has increased amounts of DHA also have better visual recognition at an earlier age. Although your Silky is already naturally smart from the DHA in her mother's milk, why not give her every advantage to become your "super puppy"?

Your Silky puppy should be portion fed each day to insure that she is eating well. Feeding your Silky a measured amount of food two to three times per day, depending on her age, also helps to control weight gain as her metabolism decreases with maturity in adulthood. Portion control is also one way to minimize the risk of your Silky "picking" at her food. When a snack is not available at all times, she learns quickly to eat the entire meal at once. This gives you a chance to regulate her feeding schedule, which also regulates potty time, making housebreaking a bit easier!

Toy breeds mature much more quickly than larger dogs, but don't tell your Silky puppy that she is a little girl. Early nutrition plays a significant role in the mental and physical condition of your Silky as she matures into adulthood.

Silky Terrier puppies benefit from a diet specially formulated for active toy breeds.

Mature Munchies

Your adult Silky Terrier, while still remaining active, playful, and on the move, has a different set of caloric requirements now that she has grown up. As she settles into adulthood, her metabolism remains more constant, without the "ups and downs" of puppy activity. A diet that is formulated to meet the needs of a healthy, active, adult dog should be the one you choose for your adult Silky Terrier. A moderate protein level is easily converted into the amino acids needed for the healthy muscles and coat of your Silky. The Silky Terrier thrives on that active lifestyle and seems to be less prone to obesity than many other toy breeds. Fatty acids in your Silky's diet are a must to insure that she develops and maintains that glamorous Silky coat.

The Right Stuff

The choice of food you offer to your Silky has a significant impact on her mental and physical well-being. Think this choice will be easy? Think again! Dog food is full of gimmicks—foods with

No two Silkys are alike when it comes to diet preferences.

different shapes, sizes, colors, and textures. There is a true smorgasbord available for the Silky Terrier palate. How do you decide what is the "pièce de résistance" for your Silky? You must first know what options are available, what is economical, and what best suits your Silky's taste buds.

Tasty Texture

Your search must begin with the texture or type of diet you wish to feed to your Silky. Diet types can be broken down into six different options, some familiar and others uncommon and hard to find.

Dry Dog Food

The most common presentation for dog food is dry dog food, or kibble. If you choose this form for your Silky Terrier, it has some definite benefits for health, and may be the most economical choice for you.

Dry foods are those containing less than 20 percent moisture. When chewed by your Silky, the hard kibble provides an abrasive action to the teeth, giving your Silky a miniature dental cleaning each time she eats a meal. The variety of shapes, sizes, and textures in dry foods offers a wide selection of options suitable for your Silky's diet. You only need to look at the number of dog food aisles at your local pet superstore to realize that there is a dry diet for every Silky Terrier, no matter what the age or activity level.

Dry dog foods are often presented at mealtime straight out of the bag. When offered alone, the dry diet lacks moisture, and the low odor that you find pleasing may make it unappetizing to your discriminating Silky Terrier.

Canned Foods

When given the option, most Silky Terriers would prefer to eat a diet that includes canned food at every meal. One look at canned foods and you will find choices that are meat only, meat with vegetables, meat with vegetables and pasta, meat with rice, and yes, even vegetarian choices. What Silky wouldn't want to have these choices?

Canned foods are very palatable due in part to their moisture content, which is greater than 65 percent. Canned foods offer an excellent addition to your Silky's dry diet, giving you the option to create a "different" taste each day by adding a new flavor. A teaspoon of the canned food of your choice, added to your Silky's dry kibble, turns that boring dry food into a tasty, tempting stew.

The soft texture of canned foods does not benefit your Silky's oral health like a dry diet can. If you allow your Silky to eat only canned diets, without the abrasive action of a dry kibble, be prepared for tartar, plaque, and bad breath!

Semimoist Diets

Semimoist foods are still available in limited choices. Semimoist diets come in packets, often resembling hamburger or cuts of meat, and may be shaped into cubes. With moisture contents between 20 percent and 64 percent, semimoist diets have quite a variation in taste. When compared to dry diets, semimoist diets have increased levels of sugar, and Silkys who are fed these diets are more susceptible to obesity.

Frozen Food

Frozen diets are available in limited areas of the United States and Canada. These diets are prepared fresh and are then frozen quickly, providing a more natural, fresher alternative to feed to your Silky. Proper preparation, storage, and thawing of these diets must be practiced to avoid feeding your Silky a diet that is contaminated.

Choosing a frozen diet can be a costly undertaking. The cost of shipping often makes it very expensive to feed, and it can be difficult to store frozen diets in any large quantity.

Freeze-dried Food

Many small dog food companies that offer frozen diets also offer a freeze-dried version of

━━━━━━━ TIP ━━━━━━━

Your Silky's Diet

When considering a diet that is not commercially prepared by a recognizable dog food company, you must understand the following:

1. If a dog food is being prepared, marketed, and sold by a small, local company, the maker may not be following the nutrient requirement guidelines set forth by the Association of American Feed Control Officials (AAFCO) or the National Research Council. Both of these organizations make sure that the larger companies are in fact providing the nutrients that are listed on each bag or can of their food.

2. Bones and Raw Food, or BARF, diets are featured in many holistic dog magazines and on web sites. Proponents of these diets feel that they more closely resemble the diets that wild dogs have eaten, and that the raw status provides a better source for usable nutrients. If these diets are not prepared carefully and stored correctly, you may be feeding raw parts that are contaminated with *Salmonella* or *E. Coli*.

3. The ingredients used to manufacture unregulated or untested diets may not be the same in any two bags or batches, leaving their nutrient status to change frequently.

their food. Freeze-dried foods are usually too expensive to feed to your Silky Terrier on any regular basis. They can make an excellent treat for training, or for that "special occasion."

Well-fed Silkys are happy, inquisitive, and always alert.

Rolled Food

Dog food that is formed and packaged in rolls, sometimes called "tube" food, is available at many pet food retailers. These foods are easily digestible and are packaged to resemble a doggie sausage. By moisture, these foods would be considered a semimoist diet; however, they do not contain large amounts of sugar. Rolled foods are offered in limited meat choices, but are highly palatable, making them one of the Silky's favorite choices. These diets are not inexpensive, however. Rolled food makes a tasty addition or topping to any dry diet and another great training treat.

Commercial or Premium Diet?

Now that you have a good idea of what type of food you want to serve to your Silky, it is time to decide where to purchase that diet. Some diets are only available through select outlets, such as veterinary clinics or pet stores. Some unique diets are only available through their manufacturer or a select few retailers. Other diets are common and can be purchased easily.

Commercially prepared diets are those diets that are mass marketed at a large number of retailers, making them readily available to you at an economical price. Commercial diets can be purchased in every grocery store, discount retailer, and feed store, and may be available from such unusual sources as your local hardware store.

Commercially prepared diets are perhaps the least expensive diet on a per bag basis. The ingredients used to prepare these diets can vary significantly with each batch or bag produced, making their nutrient content different each time you open a new bag. This can be a problem for your Silky's coat, if, for instance, the fatty acid content changes every time you change to a new bag. Commercial diets also may contain more vegetable protein sources and fillers, meaning your Silky must consume more to meet her caloric requirements. More food going in means more cleanup for you!

Premium foods are those diets marketed and sold exclusively through pet stores, grooming shops, and veterinarians. These diets contain ingredients that are of a higher quality, are more easily digestible, and often contain little or no vegetable fillers. Feeding your Silky a premium diet can actually save you money, as she will need to eat less in order to maintain the same amount of calories. The high digestibility of premium diets also means that there is less waste, resulting in an easier cleanup duty for you!

Unique diets must also be considered due to their increasing popularity among breeders and owners who are health conscious. Diets that you can cook at home from fresh, raw meats and vegetables can be an option for your Silky's diet if you are willing to prepare them correctly. If you are considering feeding a home-prepared diet, you will need to know how to properly prepare and store the diet to avoid bacterial contamination and the potential health risks to both you and your Silky Terrier.

When Good Eaters Go Bad

One of the most common complaints that the owners of toy dogs have is that their dog's once healthy appetite as a puppy gave way to that of a picky eater. Finicky Silkys are all too often created by their owners, as they were not born to be so discriminating.

It is normal for you to worry if your adult Silky misses a meal or two. Your concern may lead to "doctoring" your Silky's dinner, adding a bit of your own dinner, chicken, beef, or some other enticing morsel, in the hope it will increase her appetite. Each time your Silky experiences a better appetizer in her bowl, she is more likely to wait out her next meal to see if something better will appear.

Once your Silky begins to pick out her favorite choices, leaving the balanced food sitting in her bowl, it is very tough to change her mind about the mealtime routine. After all, refusing her food worked before, so she'll turn up her nose until you serve something better! Giving in to this blackmail produces a Silky that is no longer receiving a balanced diet. It is much easier to prevent pickiness, refraining from adding tasty tidbits to your Silky's meals. There are plenty of other taste temptations, in the form of canned diets or rolled foods, that can change the taste and even the texture of each meal.

The finicky Silky Terrier is not only frustrating to live with; this behavior can also impact your Silky's health. Her coat in particular can suffer, losing its silky appearance quickly if she does not consume a balanced diet. Picky eaters rarely consume all of the proteins, carbohydrates, and fats needed to feed the Silky Terrier attitude and health.

A short coat can be a result of poor grooming, as shown here, or a poor diet.

THE SILKY HEALTH GAME

Your Silky's health care is like a jigsaw puzzle. All the pieces must be present in the right fit to create the perfect Silky Terrier picture!

A healthy Silky Terrier is a happy Silky Terrier. Your relationship with your Silky Terrier must include another partner, the right veterinarian. Together, it will be your responsibility to insure that your Silky keeps his energetic outlook on life!

The Veterinary Team

Choosing the right veterinarian to be your Silky's primary health care provider is an extremely crucial piece of your Silky Terrier health puzzle. Remember, your Silky has a mind of his own, and he may not find the intrusion of a stranger's hands during veterinary visits a pleasant experience.

Your Silky Terrier may not require frequent visits to the veterinarian; however, it is impor-

A Silky's eyes should be bright and alert.

tant to find one who is aware of the Silky's independent, sometimes stubborn personality. Your veterinarian must also be willing to work patiently with you and must be comfortable handling the sometimes standoffish nature of the Silky. A Silky Terrier should never be treated roughly or with excessive restraint, as this only serves to aggravate the Silky attitude of "it's my world, you just live in it."

Selecting a Veterinarian

When choosing the right veterinarian for your Silky, you might want to interview several clinics before making a choice. Was the receptionist who answered the telephone friendly, or did she project the attitude that she was too busy to answer your questions? Did she seem to be knowledgeable and interested in your Silky's lifestyle? Some important questions you should ask when interviewing prospective veterinary clinics are:

1. Have your veterinarian(s) had previous experience with Silky Terriers?

2. Is one of the staff veterinarians on call to handle after-hours emergencies or do you refer your patients to an emergency clinic?

3. Does your hospital offer surgical services? Boarding or grooming for patients?

4. May I schedule a tour of your facility and meet the staff?

5. Is your hospital an American Animal Hospital Association affiliated or accredited facility?

Silky Terriers are healthy, rugged, and playful.

Remember, you need to have faith and trust in your veterinarian, as well as with the support staff that may be caring for your Silky. Your veterinarian must also respect and be willing to listen to you if your Silky's best interest is his top priority. This partnership may well last 12 or more years, so if you are afraid to ask questions or don't feel that you can communicate openly with your veterinarian, your Silky's health may ultimately be at risk.

The Veterinary Visit

At least once each year, you and your Silky should make an appointment for a friendly visit and physical exam. This yearly check-up is another important piece of the health care puzzle. Be sure to mention any unusual behaviors or problems you might have noticed, no matter how small or insignificant they might seem.

Much to the dismay of your Silky, your veterinarian will check him over from head to toe. His eyes, ears, heart, and lungs will be checked, his abdomen felt for unusual thickening or masses, and his temperature will be taken. A general health blood panel may also be suggested to monitor internal organ functions.

When your veterinarian proclaims that your Silky is in tip-top shape, your next step will be to discuss vaccinations.

Vaccines—Yes or No?

The biggest controversy in veterinary medicine today, and one of your primary concerns as a Silky Terrier owner, may be which vaccines are mandatory, yet safe enough for your pet.

We all know that vaccines have played a crucial role in minimizing the risks from such diseases as rabies, distemper, and parvovirus. But

Routine veterinary care includes a physical exam, vaccines, and parasite control.

which vaccines are really necessary, and just how often should they be given? The answer lies with an informed decision made by you and your veterinarian. Discussing your Silky's daily recreational activities and lifestyle with him, and learning what diseases may be present in your area, will help you decide which vaccinations are appropriate for your Silky Terrier. Any health concerns that your Silky is facing, such as infections or internal problems, may also factor into the decision.

Core Vaccines Versus Noncore Vaccines

Your veterinarian may suggest that your Silky receive only "core vaccines." Core vaccines are those vaccinations that are considered mandatory for public health such as rabies vaccines that prevent prevalent, life-threatening illnesses in your area, or ones that guard against diseases that are transmitted easily to humans.

If a disease is prevalent in your area, or your Silky's activities predispose him to a higher risk of contracting a specific disease, your veterinarian may want to discuss "noncore" vaccines. These vaccines are considered by many to be "elective" based on need, or for many Silkies, completely unnecessary.

Protective Titers and Duration of Immunity

Many Silky Terrier owners are well educated on today's vaccination recommendations, and you, no doubt, are one of them! Articles written about the vaccine debate often include references to vaccination titers. A vaccine titer is a

=== TIP ===

Keeping Your Silky Healthy

A general health profile monitors your Silky's internal health.

Complete Blood Count (CBC): looks at white blood cells, red blood cells, and platelets for clotting ability

Albumin: checks for liver/kidney disease

ALT: monitors liver function

Alk. Phos.: monitors liver function

Amylase: monitors pancreatic function

BUN: monitors kidney function

Creatinine: monitors kidney function

Lipase: monitors pancreatic function

Total Protein: monitors kidney/liver function

══════ TIP ══════

Core Vaccines

Distemper: Often seen in puppies with no prior vaccines; may present as an upper respiratory infection, but rapidly progresses to vomiting, diarrhea, and neurological signs (tremors).

Hepatitis: Also known as adenovirus (type 1 and 2); symptoms include liver damage, jaundice and upper respiratory infection.

Parainfluenza: A virus of the upper respiratory tract; can cause pneumonia in young or old Silky Terriers.

Parvovirus: A serious intestinal virus that causes severe vomiting, diarrhea, and fever.

Rabies: A fatal virus that affects the central nervous system and is easily transmitted to humans.

Noncore Vaccines

Bordatella: The most common cause of upper respiratory infections (kennel cough).

Coronavirus: An intestinal virus that causes vomiting and diarrhea.

Leptospirosis: A bacterial infection that causes kidney damage and failure; may be considered a "core" vaccine in some areas.

Lyme Disease: A bacterial disease contracted from a tick bite; causes fever, lethargy, and arthritic joints.

blood test that measures the amount of protective antibodies present in the body for a specific disease at the time your Silky's blood is drawn. If your Silky's protective titer level is above the "unprotected" level for the specific disease, revaccination may not be necessary at that time.

The unfortunate and confusing problem with vaccine titers is that they only give you and your veterinarian the information that your Silky's immune system is able to fight off a disease at that moment. There is no way to guarantee that the puzzle piece containing protective antibodies will last until your Silky's next veterinary visit.

Fortunately for you and your Silky, many vaccine manufacturers have been studying how long those protective antibodies may last— known as "duration of immunity." The results are still incomplete for many vaccinations, but it is now known that some vaccines that previously required a yearly shot actually provide protection for two to three years.

Safety

The modern vaccine is considered to have a large margin of safety. No vaccine can guarantee 100 percent immunity, nor can any vaccine claim to be 100 percent safe for every dog. While your Silky Terrier is not considered to be one of the breeds at high risk for a severe reaction, the toy breeds represent the highest rate of reactions overall.

If your Silky does have a vaccine reaction, he might run a slight fever or seem a bit "under the weather," lacking that determination to cause trouble. This temporary sluggish behavior will not last long. More moderate reactions might include hives, facial swelling, or panting. If any of these symptoms become evident after your Silky has received a vaccine, it is wise to call your veterinarian.

A very small percentage of toy dogs have serious reactions immediately following vaccines.

Internal Parasites

Parasite	Health Concern	Therapy/Prevention
Roundworms	Digestive health, poor nutrition; transmission to humans	Prophylactic de-worming; antiparasitic found in many heartworm preventatives
Hookworms	Digestive health, poor nutrition, anemia; transmission to humans	Monthly antiparasitic found heartworm preventatives
Whipworms	Poor nutritional health, diarrhea, weight loss	Antiparasitic must be given several times; difficult to control in soil and environment
Coccidia	Diarrhea with blood, upper respiratory symptoms, poor nutritional health	Antiprotozoal medications must be given, especially to puppies
Giardia	Diarrhea, poor weight gain	Antiprotozoal medications; often hard to diagnose
Heartworm	Decreased circulatory health, increased respiratory effort	Deep injections of antiparasitic to treat. PREVENTION IS THE KEY!

The Silky Terrier is fortunate that the terrier bloodlines in its past seem to have guarded it against a high incidence of severe, anaphylactic reactions. The remote possibility of weakness, shortness of breath, tremors, and collapse are still a concern when vaccinating any toy breed, including your Silky.

There are many factors that must be considered, and open dialogue with your veterinarian must occur when fitting the pieces of the vaccine puzzle.

Parasites

Nothing can affect your Silky Terrier's mental and physical health as quickly or as quietly as hosting an uninvited parasite party. Some parasites are internal, living silently within your Silky and affecting his digestive, circulatory, and immune health. Other parasites are external, wreaking havoc on your Silky's beautiful skin and coat and potentially transmitting life-threatening illnesses.

The types of internal and external parasites that await your Silky, and how prevalent they may be, can vary from one location to the next. To help complete your health care puzzle, a stool sample should be checked during your Silky's yearly check-up, to ensure that he has not become an unsuspecting host. Although it may be hard to convince your Silky to cooperate, if your area is affected by heartworm disease, he should also have a blood test each year to be sure he is free from this parasite.

External Parasites

Parasite	Health Concern	Therapy/Prevention
Fleas	Skin lesions, may bite humans; transmission of bubonic plague	Treat with parasiticide, monthly topical preventative
Ticks	Skin lesions, may bite humans; transmission of several life-threatening illness to humans	Treat with parasiticide, remove tick, monthly preventative
Sarcoptes mites	Chronic scratching, skin lesions, hair loss; may bite humans	Treat with parasiticidal agents at veterinary clinic only
Demodicosis mites	Patchy hair loss, leads to secondary infections	Treat with parasiticidal agents at veterinary clinic

Many parasites may also enjoy sharing your home with you and your Silky. Most internal parasites shed eggs into the outdoor environment where your Silky spends a great deal of his playtime, and external pests such as fleas and ticks share this outdoor living space. If your home becomes a "parasite palace," ask your veterinarian for advice on how to treat your Silky and his home environment. There is a risk of transmission of many parasites to you and your family. Most parasites can be easily prevented, and while it may not be a pleasant task, parasite prevention for your Silky should be a priority. Your Silky, as well as your family, thanks you!

No Unwanted Puppies! Spay or Neuter Your Silky

The final health puzzle piece, and perhaps one of the most important, is whether or not to surgically render your Silky Terrier incapable of reproduction. In females, this procedure is called a "spay" or ovariohysterectomy. In males, the procedure is known as a "neuter" or castration.

The reasons *not* to breed your Silky are quite numerous. First, Silkys who have been "altered" typically live longer, healthier lives by eliminating the risk of malignant tumors of the reproductive organs. In neutered male Silkys, the incidence of malignant rectal tumors is lowered, and the tendency to wander in search of "Mrs. Right" is decreased. Neutering may also reduce some of the assertive behavior that can be troublesome when living with a Silky. Spaying your female will eliminate the nuisance of "heat cycles," reduce the likelihood that she will develop mammary cancer, as well as eliminate the possibility of an unwanted pregnancy.

Your veterinarian can discuss the best time to perform the procedure for your Silky. Most veterinarians and Silky breeders agree that the surgery should be scheduled between the ages of six months and one year of age, and before a female's first heat cycle.

Microchips and Your Silky Terrier

If your Silky Terrier should wander away from home, how would you positively identify him? A microchip can now be implanted in your Silky Terrier to give you an easy way to identify your Silky should he become lost.

This tiny chip, implanted between the shoulder blades, contains a number that is unique to your Silky Terrier. Once implanted, you should then register your Silky's name, along with your name, address, and phone numbers, with the microchip's manufacturer. Additional information is also requested, such as your veterinarian's information, should the manufacturer be unable to locate you when your Silky is found.

If your Silky should be unfortunate enough to be impounded, he will be scanned and the microchip information retrieved. Animal shelters and veterinary clinics then use that information to track you down and reunite you with your Silky.

Having your veterinarian implant a microchip during a surgical procedure is an excellent time to safeguard your Silky from becoming missing in action! Anesthesia is not required, as your Silky will feel no different from when he receives his vaccinations.

Silky Terrier Health Problems

The Silky Terrier has a stellar reputation when it comes to health issues. Much of this credit is owed to the dedicated individuals who, as Silky Terrier breeders, give you another piece of the puzzle by making health concerns a top priority when planning a breeding.

When compared to many other toy breeds, the list of health problems and diseases that poten-

Silky Terrier puppies are adorable, but spaying or neutering keeps them healthier in the long run.

tially face the Silky Terrier owner is relatively short. No breed, whether purebred, "designer dog," or "Heinz 57," can be guaranteed to be free of health problems. Genetic testing or screening may be possible for some of the diseases that affect the Silky Terrier; however, other problems have no definite cause or genetic test available to help Silky breeders and owners.

Health Problems and the Young Silky Terrier

The Silky Terrier has several health problems that can surface during the first few months to first year of life; however, the incidence of serious health concerns seems to be relatively low when compared to many other toy breeds.

Hydrocephalus

As with many of the toy breeds, the Silky Terrier can be afflicted with this neurological condition. The brain is composed of a series of spaces or ventricles, which are occupied by cerebrospinal fluid (CSF). If there is an increase in the production of CSF, or a slower than normal reabsorption rate, the ventricles may become filled with too much fluid. This excess causes increased pressure within the brain, resulting in damage to sensitive tissue over time. Most cases of hydrocephalus in the Silky Terrier are present shortly after birth, known as congenital hydrocephalus. Hydrocephalus that is mild may go undetected until your Silky Terrier faces some other health crisis such as stress, disease, or injury.

The symptoms of hydrocephalus include tremors, seizures, "slow" or "dull" movements, and

Silky Terrier puppies suffer from very few genetic concerns.

a decreased ability to learn simple tasks. Visual problems may also be evident in severe cases.

If your veterinarian suspects hydrocephalus, he may recommend an MRI or CT scan to be sure his diagnosis is correct. There is no popular, effective treatment for your Silky if he is hydrocephalic, although steroid therapy to reduce brain swelling and diuretics to help absorb excess CSF may be prescribed and may help to alleviate some symptoms.

Luxating Patellas

The active nature of your Silky Terrier can be affected by a condition in which the patella, or kneecap, temporarily dislocates. Patellar luxation is typically a problem that is not present at birth, as the condition often develops during a growth spurt. Patellar luxation is typically seen in the Silky Terrier between four months and one year of age. During this growth period, the groove in which the kneecap sits may become too shallow, or the tendons that secure it may become unable to stabilize the patella. With each movement of the affected leg, the kneecap shifts, causing your Silky discomfort and temporary instability of the joint. One or both of your Silky's rear legs may be affected.

Patellar luxation is graded based on the severity of the lameness. Grade I luxation is intermittent or infrequent, with the leg temporarily carried. Grade II luxation causes symptoms more frequently. The leg is "tucked up" under your Silky's belly much of the time when he is running. Grade III and Grade IV luxations are both characterized by a permanent displacement of the patella and a recognizable inability to place

Seizures

Watching your first seizure is frightening! The Silky may become stiff and whine or whimper. Convulsions may result in the release of urine and/or stool.

If your Silky experiences a seizure, remain calm and try to darken the room and eliminate noise. Do not try to reach into your Silky's mouth or grab his tongue. Talk to him in a soothing tone of voice until the seizure ends.

He may be confused or sluggish following each seizure and may not return to normal for some time.

weight on the affected leg. Both Grade III and Grade IV luxations will require surgery to stabilize the joint. If your Silky has been diagnosed with one of the lower grades, he may require daily medication to minimize his pain from the joint changes over time. Luxating patellas are considered to be hereditary in many cases, so your Silky should not be bred if he is diagnosed with this orthopedic problem.

Legg-Calvés Perthes

Legg-Calvés Perthes is another orthopedic condition that can affect your young Silky Terrier. Legg-Calvés Perthes is the necrosis, or destruction of the head of the femur, as the result of poor or decreased blood supply during the development of the joint. This disease affects the Silky Terrier during growth, with the average age of diagnosis being six to ten

months of age. It is common for only one rear leg to be affected in the Silky Terrier; however, the disease can affect both rear legs.

The first symptom of this painful disease is a limp that gets more severe over a short period of time. As the bone deteriorates, pain in the leg may become more evident. If your Silky has Legg-Calvés Perthes and it is left untreated, the femoral head can fracture and cause severe pain.

Your veterinarian may recommend surgery to remove the femoral head completely, an excellent option for treating this disease. The majority of Silky Terriers who have this surgery live normal, active lives. Legg-Calvés Perthes may have a hereditary component, so it would be wise to let your Silky's breeder know that your Silky is affected, and have him neutered at the appropriate time.

Health Concerns of the Adult Silky Terrier

Your Silky has celebrated his first birthday! Now that he is an adult, most of the health problems he might face are considered to be easily managed.

Seizure Disorder

Seizures, also known as idiopathic epilepsy, are seen occasionally in some bloodlines of the Silky Terrier. Most often, Silky Terriers experience their first seizure between one year and three years of age. If your Silky experiences a seizure, you should contact your veterinarian immediately. She may want to run a comprehensive blood panel to rule out a problem with your Silky's internal organs as the cause. Other causes may be explored, such as any known exposure to toxins, internal parasites, or accidental ingestion of medications or plants.

If no specific cause can be found for the seizure, idiopathic epilepsy can be considered. Anti-seizure medication may be recommended if your Silky has frequent seizures or they are long in duration. These medications can reduce the frequency or duration of seizures, and in some cases, eliminate seizures completely.

If your Silky has been diagnosed with seizure disorder, your veterinarian will advise you how to monitor your Silky at home. She will continue to monitor your Silky's organ functions each year with a follow-up blood panel.

Skin Problems

Skin and coat problems in the adult Silky Terrier are a more frequently reported concern. While the diseases that affect the Silky are not considered "major" problems, arriving at the correct diagnosis and the subsequent treatment can be a costly nuisance for you, the Silky Terrier owner.

Color dilution alopecia frequently affects the adult Silky Terrier. This condition is characterized by progressive hair loss in areas where the coat color is unusually light or an abnormal color. Your Silky's once beautiful coat may begin to look thinner along the sides or legs, and while this hair loss is not considered to be a problem, the areas affected may also be more prone to bacterial infections.

Allergic dermatitis, commonly referred to as allergies, affects many breeds, and the Silky Terrier is no exception. Allergies, simply put, are extreme sensitivities to any substance, known as an allergen. Allergies can be one of the most frustrating conditions for both you and your Silky, as they cannot be cured, only controlled.

The symptoms of allergies, intense itching and redness of the skin, lead to scratching and self-trauma. Secondary bacterial infections and hair loss are not uncommon when allergic symptoms are present.

Determining the cause, or allergen, can be difficult, and allergies are often misdiagnosed. A visit to a dermatologist for you and your often miserable Silky, and subsequent allergy testing, will help assess the underlying allergen(s). Once the allergens have been identified, allergy shots may be given in an effort to reduce your Silky's symptoms. Antihistamines may be used or oral steroids prescribed to temporarily alleviate itching.

Seborrhea also affects the Silky Terrier. Seborrhea is commonly thought of as a dry, flaky skin condition; however, there are several different forms of seborrhea. Some result in dryness or flaking, while others may cause scaliness or greasiness.

Seborrhea is actually an abnormal acceleration in the rate of the normal skin cell cycle. This increased rate of skin loss causes thickening of the skin, abnormal scaling, and also predisposes those affected areas to bacterial and yeast infections. Seborrhea is generally the result of some underlying medical problem, so if your Silky has been diagnosed with seborrhea, he may have some other underlying medical condition, such as allergic dermatitis, hypothyroidism, parasitic problems, or poor nutrition.

To treat seborrhea, proper diagnosis and treatment of the underlying medical cause is the first step in controlling seborrhea. Routine bathing with an appropriate shampoo (as prescribed by your veterinarian) is paramount in slowing the skin cell cycle and managing this disease.

Endocrine Problems

Endocrine diseases can affect dogs of all sizes and breeds, including your adult Silky. The endocrine system is responsible for secreting a variety of hormones throughout your Silky's little body. When those hormones are secreted incorrectly, resulting in levels that are too high or too low, a disease process may result. Tumors of either the pituitary glands or adrenal glands can cause an overproduction of cortisol, your Silky's own natural form of cortisone, creating a condition known as hyperadrenocorticism or Cushing's disease.

Cushing's disease affects the middle-aged Silky Terrier, and you may not even recognize the early symptoms. Skin diseases, which are often the first signs of trouble, are not often attributed to an endocrine problem. Thinning hair is often the first recognizable symptom, although you might notice an increased thirst, more frequent urination, or a slight increase in your Silky's appetite.

Diagnosing hyperadrenocorticism can be tricky for your veterinarian. Specific levels of several hormones must be measured over a specific time frame. By measuring cortisol in your Silky's bloodstream as a baseline, and then either stimulating or suppressing the adrenal system and measuring the resulting levels of cortisol, Cushing's disease can be further suspected or ruled out.

Cushing's disease can be fairly simple to control with one of several different medications, which your veterinarian can prescribe. If your Silky is diagnosed with this disease, he might be more susceptible to infections due to a lower immune system.

Visual Problems

One disease that has been recently diagnosed in the Silky Terrier with increasing frequency is progressive retinal atrophy, or PRA. PRA is a hereditary condition that initially affects your Silky's ability to see during periods of dim light (night blindness). As the disease progresses, all

Properly maintaining your Silky's coat will lesson the chance for skin problems.

vision in the affected eye begins to fail, and the pupil may become noticeably dilated. A cataract may form as the disease reaches its end stage.

Progressive retinal atrophy is an eye disease that occurs in the older adult Silky. Most Silky owners don't notice the loss of vision at first, as the Silky is very good at adapting to its circumstances and surroundings. It isn't until your Silky begins to have trouble with his daytime vision, or the eye becomes slightly cloudy, that you may begin to suspect a problem. Many owners believe that their Silky may be suffering from "cataracts" due to his advancing age. These owners often fail to seek veterinary help, and unfortunately the disease is never diagnosed.

Eye diseases must often be diagnosed and treated by a veterinary ophthalmologist. In order to diagnose PRA, your Silky will have to allow his pupils to be dilated and an exam of the rods and cones in the eye to be performed with a special instrument. While any cataract that has formed may be treated, there is no treatment currently available to restore your Silky's vision and slow the progression of PRA.

SHAPING YOUR SILKY

Silky Terriers love to be in control. Without constant guidance and direction from you, your Silky will have you trained in no time!

It is no secret that a well-behaved Silky Terrier makes a great family pet. It is unfortunate that all too often Silky Terrier owners see behaviors that they do not like, yet they do very little to change them. Making excuses or complaining about your Silky's bad habits will not change those behaviors. You must learn to recognize your Silky's bad behaviors early, and have a training plan that will allow you to turn them into good behaviors. Training your Silky to have manners will make her more relaxed both at home and as she explores the world around her.

Train, Don't Complain

Training your Silky to be the best she can be is a constant work in progress. Shaping her behavior is not an exact science—it is more sim-

Your Silky should learn to quietly pay attention to you.

ilar to creating a work of art that is molded and changed until you have a beautiful masterpiece. Of course, your Silky will have her own opinion on what is acceptable behavior, and she will try very hard to convince you that her bad behavior has some merit! Teaching your Silky can be a battle if, from your Silky's perspective, the techniques you choose are too forceful or without a clearly identifiable benefit, so be prepared to change your strategy if your training is not moving in a positive direction.

Training Techniques

You have already learned that your Silky Terrier has a mind of her own. When it comes to teaching her manners or correcting her tantrums, you will need to decide just how to get through to her without creating additional problems.

Shaping your Silky will be impossible if you only use harsh, physical tactics. She will learn your expectations more quickly, and be able to perfect good behavior, if you understand how she learns and use balanced techniques to shape her behavior.

Your Silky believes that most of the time the world revolves around her. Life is all about what works for her to get things done her way. Each time she wants something, or has an idea of how she wants something to be, she will behave in a way that produces that result. Each time your Silky does a behavior, there is a consequence. The resulting consequence of any behavior can be either good or bad. To your Silky, any reward for a behavior, or getting what she wants, is a good consequence. Behaviors that are rewarded will then be repeated. If that same behavior results in something unpleasant occurring as a consequence, or your Silky does not get what she wanted, she is more likely to try a different behavior next time.

It will be much easier to live with your Silky each day if you remember to stay on top of her behavior early, providing good consequences or rewards for the behaviors you want her to repeat. Correcting the behaviors you do not want to see repeated, making the results of her action unpleasant or non-beneficial, will change her mind about her behavior in a way that does not involve a confrontation or battle.

The Learning Curve

Every Silky Terrier should have excellent manners around other animals, and yours in no exception. Well-behaved Silkys are model canine citizens and can visit with other dogs and enjoy the company of friends and neighbors. You should begin to teach your Silky "the basics" as early as possible, and yes, even old Silkys can learn new tricks! Once you see how

easy it is to positively motivate your Silky, there is no limit to what your Silky can learn.

Attention, Please!

Reliably getting your Silky's attention when you need it the most is perhaps one of the biggest challenges for Silky owners to overcome. Your Silky must learn that when you say her name, or ask her to look at you, there is great joy and reward for performing this simple task.

Try this simple test to see if your Silky finds you interesting and rewarding. The next time your Silky is distracted, chewing on a favorite bone or playing with a toy, say her name ONCE in a normal tone of voice. What is her reaction? Did she acknowledge your voice by turning her ears, look at you, or come bounding toward you? Or did she completely ignore her name, preferring instead to continue to reward herself

Begin with Basics

Here are some commands every Silky Terrier owner should teach his or her Silky:

WATCH	SIT	DOWN	COME
HEEL	STAY	LEAVE IT	WAIT
DROP IT	QUIET	BEDTIME	MOVE IT

by playing with that toy? Because of their independent nature, most Silkys will only give a slight acknowledgment that they heard their name at all. That self-assurance can lead to defiance, so you need to positively change her outlook when you say her name.

Your goal should be that when you say your Silky's name, her response is always to immediately come and find you to see what you wanted.

Step 1. Begin at a close distance to your Silky. With an appropriate food reward in hand, say your Silky's name once, and remain quiet and unmoving. Watch for any sign that she heard your voice, such as a turn of her ears, head turn in your direction, or pause in activity. Verbally reward any acknowledgment, no matter how small, with a *"Good girl."* If she comes toward you, get excited and continue to verbally reward any movement in your direction. If she reaches you, she gets a *BONUS* food reward! Remember, that was the goal!

Step 2. Repeat the exercise several times each day at home. The level of excitement in your voice directly affects how quickly your Silky will return to you, so don't be afraid to sound thrilled that your Silky is coming to find you.

Step 3. As your Silky begins to run toward you each time she hears her name, increase the distance from which you begin the exercise. You can even try it from an adjacent room, hidden from view, when finding you at a larger distance is no problem.

Step 4. Begin to do the same exercise with your Silky on leash while in different locations that have added distractions. Your yard can be an excellent place to test your Silky's response. As the distraction level increases, go back to saying her name at a close distance, and be certain that you immediately verbally reward any look toward you. Bonus rewards might also need to be "better," or more appealing, in order for your Silky to come to you instead of chasing birds!

Train your Silky to have excellent manners.

The Sit

The *sit* command is the foundation for many other exercises that your Silky should learn. *Sit* should be taught to your Silky early and used each day to remind your Silky that she needs to consider you a leader. Ask your Silky to *"sit"* in front of every door, so that it will open; a *sit* can become the only way to get her food bowl to move down to the floor at mealtime. These "life rewards" re-emphasize the command on a daily basis and remind your Silky that nothing in life is free!

Step 1. To begin teaching the *sit* command, find a food reward that really motivates your Silky. With the reward in your hand, start by telling your Silky the command *"Sit,"* and move the treat from the tip of your Silky's nose, just over her head between her ears, and over her

back toward her tail. When her head lifts up to follow the treat, her rear end should tuck under her into the *sit* position. Reward her immediately with verbal praise, followed by the food reward. Repeat this exercise two additional times.

Step 2. If your Silky jumps up for the food, you might be holding it too high above her head, or moving it too quickly over her head and back. Withdraw your hand from your Silky if she jumps up, and wait a moment before trying again.

Step 3. Once your Silky is performing the exercise quickly, it is time to reduce the need for a food lure. Begin to reward the *sit* randomly by verbally rewarding every successful *sit,* and bonus rewarding with the food reward at random times.

Watch Me

Getting your Silky Terrier to look at you is one thing—keeping her attention focused on you for even a short period of time can be quite another. A practical reason for this exercise is that if your Silky is focused intently on you, she cannot get into trouble, and this goes against the very nature of a Silky Terrier's background. Therefore, watching you must mean a big reward at first, as it is a big world out there, and there are so many other things for a Silky to get focused on! The *watch me* exercise can be one of your best tools for changing barking behaviors in your Silky, so do not skip this training exercise.

Step 1. Ask your Silky to *"Sit"* directly in front of you and verbally reward the correct response. Using a food reward in your hand,

To teach the "sit" command, find a reward that really interests your Silky.

gently touch your Silky's nose, say the command *"Watch me,"* and slowly bring your hand straight up to the bridge of your nose between your eyes. As your Silky's head lifts up to follow the food lure, verbally reward the response quietly and then give her the food reward. Repeat this exercise two additional times.

Step 2. As your Silky's response to look up at you becomes automatic, begin to increase the time she must look at you before you give her the food reward. Start out by counting silently to three, and reward her if she is still watching. Increase the time to five seconds if she is successful. Continue to increase the time in small amounts for each successful *watch me.*

Step 3. If your Silky looks away during the exercise, repeat the *"Watch me"* command and, if necessary, gently touch her nose again to allow her the chance to focus on you again. Immediately reward the *watch* and try again. If your Silky continues to look away, the distractions might be too great, and you will need

If your Silky is focused on you, she is not getting into trouble.

to go back to rewarding the correct behavior more frequently.

Step 4. Once your Silky can hold a *watch me* look for thirty seconds or more with minimal distractions, begin to practice this exercise with bigger distractions. Remember to shorten the time between the command *"Watch me"* and the reward at first, to make paying attention to you more beneficial than checking out the distractions that surround your Silky.

Down

Asking a Silky Terrier to lie down in one spot is equivalent to asking her to completely shut off her tenacious personality. The *down* position is one of relaxation, something your Silky may find completely unnecessary unless she has joined you on the couch for an evening of television.

Your Silky needs to learn, however, that at times you might expect her to quiet down and

---

TIP

More Training Tips

A food reward used to move your Silky into position is called a LURE.

A hand signal and a verbal word for an exercise are both CUES.

When teaching a new exercise, use both lures and cues to help your Silky learn more quickly.

Doing each new exercise three times in a row successfully may also help your Silky Terrier perfect behaviors quickly.

relax. Lying down on a rug can become your Silky's routine while you enjoy dinner or the only way to make a game of ball chasing happen!

Step 1. Begin with your Silky in the *sit* position. With a food reward in your hand, give your Silky the command *"Down"* and move your hand from her nose down between her front legs toward her stomach. As her nose follows the food lure under her belly, she should fold into the *down* position. As soon as her elbows are on the floor, verbally reward this response and let her have the food treat.

Step 2. If your Silky does not fold into the *down* position, preferring to "pop up" into a standing position, ask her to *sit* again, and repeat the *"Down"* command. Try to lure her again by moving the treat under her front legs.

Step 3. If luring her under her front legs does not produce a *down* response, try moving the treat from her nose, to the floor between her legs, and then back toward you in an "L" shape.

Your Silky Terrier should learn that lying down can be a rewarding position.

Step 4. The *down* exercise may take a while for your Silky to learn and perfect. It is important that you do not get frustrated or try to force her into position. She will get it eventually, and by doing it on her own, will perfect the exercise much more quickly.

Come Here

The *come* command is the one behavior every Silky Terrier needs to learn. It is also the hardest command for her to perfect, frustrating impatient Silky Terrier owners. Teaching your Silky to return to you every time you give the command *"Come"* should be a priority, as the very nature of your Silky, inquisitive and fearless, often propels her into situations that can be potentially life threatening.

If you have practiced the attention exercise, your Silky already has a foundation for a reliable recall, or *come.* You must take steps to ensure that you don't destroy that desire to come back to you quickly, and continue to reward your Silky when she does return, making her believe that you are the center of her universe when she hears that magic word *"come."*

Step 1. Let's begin by playing a game that involves big food rewards for the right response. Ask a family member to help you; have her stand at a 15- or 20-foot distance from you (a hallway or open room in your home is great for this exercise).

Next, say your Silky's name and the command *"Come,"* and as soon as she starts toward you, begin to praise her in a high-pitched tone of voice. You can pat your legs, clap your hands, or use any other method to let your Silky know that you are excited about her motion toward you. As soon as she reaches you, tell her *"Good girl"* and give her the food reward.

Step 2. As soon as your Silky has her food reward, stand up straight and have the helper say your Silky's name, followed by the command *"Come"* as soon as she turns to look his way. He should get excited as well, and give her the food reward when she reaches him.

Step 3. Repeat this exercise several times to see how quickly your Silky begins to love this game. Each time she hears her name followed by the word *"Come"* she should now be flying toward you. You can then begin to do this exercise outside in a secure area, where the distractions are greater. Remember, you will need to be more attractive to your Silky than the distractions that surround her, and your food reward may need to be of greater value.

Step 4. Once she has learned this game and is quickly returning to you each time she is called, you can begin to practice the recall when you are with her alone and she is on a leash. Allow her to go to the end of the leash and get slightly distracted, say her name and the *"Come"* command. If she does not immediately begin to return to you, start to back away from her and get excited when she starts toward you. Verbally reward her, and follow up with a food reward for catching up to you.

Walk This Way

Your well-behaved, social Silky should walk quietly and calmly along your side, enjoying your time together. Unfortunately, her desire to be involved in every activity that surrounds her often overrides incomplete training, and she pulls at the end of the leash in an effort to quickly get where she thinks she needs to be.

Selecting the Right Tools for Training

✔ Collars: Several different types are available and each has a different purpose.

Buckle collar: A great everyday collar for your Silky to be fitted with his ID tags.

Choke collar: Considered a training collar, choke collars give a slight correction by applying pressure to the neck when used properly.

Pinch collar: A pinch or prong collar is a training aid used by some trainers on difficult or out of control dogs. The prongs apply a deeper pressure when fitted properly and used correctly.

✔ Head Collars: Sometimes referred to as head halters, head collars offer a gentle alternative to help control the overactive Silky.

✔ Harness: A harness is a great way to walk your Silky if he has a neck problem or will not accept a collar. Harnesses are a poor choice for the Silky who already pulls his owner.

✔ Leash: Your leash is your "connection" to your Silky during training. There are several varieties.

Training lead: Available in two lengths, 4 foot and 6 foot. They are available in both leather and nylon.

Flexible lead: Retractable leads are available in longer lengths. While they are wonderful to allow your Silky more room to roam, they are difficult to use for training.

She may also announce her arrival by barking at every animate object along the way!

The tone for a walk with your Silky is set with the first few steps you take. The first few minutes after you exit your front door are very important if you intend to have a relaxed, quiet walk with your Silky. If you allow her to lead, pulling and tugging at the end of the leash, she will pull until she gets wherever she wants to go. If you take away any benefit to the pulling behavior, by either stopping or moving away from an object that she expresses interest in, you can change the pulling behavior and begin to enjoy walking with your Silky.

Before you begin each walk, you must decide where you want your Silky to be. The universal

Your Silky has a natural curiosity, so learning to return to you on command is important.

heel position is with your Silky along your leg on your left side. To begin, your leash should be hanging with enough slack to give it a "fish hook" appearance. If the leash becomes tighter during your walk, the slack seeming to disappear quickly, your Silky is out of position, probably walking too far in front of you and pulling. If you allow your Silky to pull, she quickly learns that this behavior is acceptable and normal, and it is much more difficult to use your leash and collar to correct this behavior if there is no slack in the leash.

Teaching your Silky to walk in proper *heel position* is much easier if you can keep her attention on your walk, by rewarding her if she looks at you as you are moving forward. Using an enticing food reward to focus your Silky's attention on you, and rewarding each time she holds that gaze during a walk, is an excellent way to teach her this behavior. If you hold your leash in your left hand, it is much easier to keep her attention focused on you by using your right hand to hold the food reward, and wiggling your fingers slightly out in front of her as you move. As she looks at your "moving target," hoping for a food reward, begin to move it in toward your stomach, which pulls her gaze up toward you and away from distractions.

Step 1. With your Silky sitting on your left side, get her attention by saying her name. When she looks at you, say *"Heel"* and begin to move forward at a normal pace. If she bolts to the end of the leash in an effort to pull, STOP. Do not say anything to her and do not tug on the leash. When she turns her head to look at you, pat your left leg and tell her *"Back"* and coax her back into heel position. Once she is back along your left side, you can repeat the command to *"Heel"* and begin to go forward. As long as she remains in position, you can continue to move forward. If your Silky forges ahead again, do not move forward.

Step 2. If you are diligent in stopping when your Silky sets her mind to pulling, it won't be long before she walks more calmly alongside you. Once she has a better idea of where you expect her to be, if she moves forward out of position, you can give her a leash correction by pulling the leash back sharply and verbally using the command *"Back."* Praise her for slowing down and returning to *heel position*.

Step 3. Using a moving target to focus your Silky is an excellent way to pass distractions such as squirrels, rabbits, other dogs, and people. As you begin to approach the object, you will need to reward your Silky much more quickly when she looks at you. Do not reward her if she is looking away!

Step 4. Another great way to teach your Silky to focus is by turning away from an object if she pulls toward it. A sharp "about turn" is an effective correction, and takes away any benefit to your Silky who is pulling toward an object. Walk far enough away from the distraction until your Silky begins to focus on you again, and then turn back and walk toward it as a reward. If she pulls again, quickly turn away and praise her when she is walking along your left side. The more you practice this strategy, the faster she will learn that pulling has no benefit.

Stay Put

The Silky Terrier that remains in one spot, glued there until she is told to move, is a rarity.

Enjoying a quiet walk together!

It is a big world out there, and your Silky believes that if she hangs around any one place too long she will miss something important. Her keen hearing can also be a problem, as she feels that every little noise must be investigated. Staying in one spot at your request must be continually worked on, starting out for a very short period of time, and building up to a longer time frame. If you are going to really teach this exercise, don't allow your Silky to "cheat" by moving just before you were going to give her the okay to move. If she learns that you are not really serious about her staying put, she won't take the command seriously, and will begin to take advantage of you whenever she thinks she can!

Step 1. The *stay* exercise should always be started on leash. Ask your Silky to *sit* in front of you. Verbally reward the response, and give the

Learning to "sit and stay" is important for puppies and adults alike.

command *"Stay"* while at the same time use the outstretched, flat palm of your hand like a "stop sign" to signal that you expect her to remain in position. Take one step backwards, wait a second or two, and then step back in front of your sitting Silky. Wait a second before you give your Silky the okay to get up, with a release word such as *"Free,"* and praise her for remaining in position.

Step 2. If your Silky gets up when you step backwards, jerk the leash straight up toward her head as you verbally correct her with a stern *"No."* Make sure your leash is not too tight and that you didn't accidentally pull her forward as you stepped away. Ask her to *sit* again, verbally reward the response, and repeat the *stay* command and hand signal.

Step 3. Once your Silky Terrier has figured out that *"Stay"* means that she should not move, you can begin to increase *either* the length of time for the *stay* or the distance between you and your Silky. Do not attempt to increase both at the same time. You may also want to try the *stay* exercise with your Silky in the *down* position. Be ready to correct her if she "pops up" as you stand up! This is a common problem with adding *stay* to the *down* command.

Step 4. If you believe that your Silky truly has mastered the idea, meaning she can do a *sit and stay* consistently at home, you should begin to practice this exercise outside or in an area with some distractions. You will need to decrease the time and perhaps even the distance each time your distractions increase.

Training Troubles

It is much easier to prevent bad behaviors from turning into bad habits, but sometimes, in spite of your best efforts, your Silky may behave poorly. Correcting bad behaviors that your Silky believes are necessary or finds enjoyable can be a challenge. Timing your corrections to occur when the bad behavior is actually occurring is critical to the success of changing your Silky's bad behavior. Remember that a correction is only effective if it changes the behavior when given a minimal number of times!

There are two ways to approach changing your Silky's behavior. When you see a behavior you would love to change, ask yourself if you can provide a correction that will quickly and effectively change your Silky's bad behavior. Using a shaker can or bark collar to stop inappropriate barking would be an example of corrections that can be used at the proper time to quickly change a behavior.

If you cannot administer an effective correction for a behavior, can you take away what your Silky wants that triggered the behavior? Can you remove any benefit your Silky gets from the specific behavior? Jumping up to greet you or your visitors can be quickly stopped if you take away the benefit your Silky gets by jumping. As much as we believe we are correcting her by telling her "No," pushing her down or talking to her only reinforces the behavior. Petting her or talking to her only when she has all four feet firmly on the floor teaches her that the interaction she wants only occurs when she is well behaved.

Seeking Professional Help

Enrolling your Silky in an obedience class is an excellent way to begin to teach your Silky Terrier how to behave. Silky Terrier puppies will

========= TIP =========

Selecting the Right Tools for Training

Dog training has evolved in recent years, and with it comes a host of new training tools and aids.

✔ **Clicker:** a fun positive way to give a reward.

✔ **Remote collars:** Training collars that correct behaviors with a sound, spray, or electric stimulus.

✔ **Fence systems:** Electronic fence containment systems combine a warning sound with an electric stimulus.

benefit from a Kindergarten Puppy Class, or KPT, where basic manners are taught, with some emphasis placed on social skills as well. Adult Silkys often enjoy the activity of a Beginners Obedience Class.

You might feel more comfortable working with a professional dog trainer who visits your home. Personal trainers can offer one-on-one instruction, but access to working around other dogs is generally limited.

Whether you choose a class environment for your Silky or a professional, in-home trainer, it is important that you are comfortable with the training style and methods of the instructor. You should visit a class to watch how the instructor interacts with both the owners and their dogs, or ask for references before you sign up with an in-home instructor. Your veterinarian may be able to provide you with a list of suitable classes or trainers in your area.

THE SUCCESSFUL SILKY TERRIER

Every Silky Terrier has a job—a special purpose to which he devotes his energy and attention. For some Silkys, their job description may be a bit different—channeling that terrier tenacity into a Silky success story.

On the Job

The Silky Terrier is a unique breed, well suited for many tasks. These tasks might focus on the beauty of the Silky Terrier. Some combine the quick, responsive nature of the Silky with fun, agile games. Still others test the strong instinct of the Silky to rid its home of vermin, a behavior reminiscent of its Australian Terrier roots.

If you are looking for something different to try, an activity both you and your Silky can conquer, why not explore the possibilities? Your Silky has the ability to excel at many things, and often the desire to attempt any task you put before him.

Silky Terriers are a breed of many talents.

Conformation

Conformation is the beauty pageant of dog events. Dog shows have become extravagant events, televised on many major networks. Exhibiting a Silky in conformation is a way to evaluate your Silky for its breeding potential. A Silky who attains his American Kennel Club Championship is often considered worthy of future consideration for breeding.

At every dog show, male Silkys, or dogs, are judged first, followed by the females, or bitches. Championship points are awarded to the winner of the dog classes and the bitch classes, based on the number of that sex that are in competition on that day. A championship is earned by accumulating a total of fifteen points, with at least two wins being major wins, with point totals of three, four, or five.

An active Silky is a happy Silky.

No more than five points can be awarded at any single event.

A conformation judge examines each Silky and compares him or her to the Silky Terrier Club of America breed standard. The Silky who best meets that standard is awarded Best of Breed, and moves on to further competition in the Toy Group.

In order to be eligible for conformation competition, your Silky must be fully registered with the American Kennel Club (AKC) and must meet the majority of the criteria in the breed standard. Silkys that are surgically altered are ineligible to compete in conformation.

Obedience Competition

Competing in obedience can be a great way to combine your need to establish and maintain leadership with your Silky's inquisitive nature. Many obedience exercises require a bit of thinking on your Silky's part, and it gives him a series of tasks to focus on and learn.

There are many different levels of obedience competition. This variety provides a level suitable for nearly every Silky Terrier owner. Spayed and neutered Silkys are welcome and encouraged to compete, and if your Silky was sold on a limited registration, he is also eligible for obedience competition.

Rally Obedience

Rally is the newest addition to obedience competition and a great place to start for any Silky Terrier and his owner. Rally takes a fun approach to obedience, where encouraging your Silky with verbal praise and hand cues is allowed.

Scoring is based on your Silky's performance, and deductions are taken for mistakes in each exercise. The time it takes to complete the course may also be used to break tie scores. Three qualifying scores of 70 points or better, out of a possible 100 points, earn your Silky a Rally title.

There are three levels of Rally competition. The novice exercises are all done on leash, while advanced and excellent courses are completed off leash. Advanced and excellent courses also combine more advanced training with obstacles such as jumps.

Novice Obedience

Your next step after Rally may be the novice obedience ring. Novice obedience contains both on-leash heeling and off-leash heeling, and demonstrates your Silky's ability to stay in place while sitting, lying down, and standing. A recall exercise, for your Silky to show that he can come to you when called, is also included in the Novice obedience ring. Points are deducted for mistakes in each exercise. Three qualifying scores of 170 points or better, out of a possible 200 points, earn your Silky the title of Companion Dog, or CD.

Open Obedience

The Open obedience competition is performed strictly off leash and takes dedication and perseverance on your part, in order to teach your Silky Terrier to perform this job. The Open competition combines off-leash heeling with jumps and retrieving. The recall exercise

━━━━━━━━━ TIP ━━━━━━━━━

The Competitive Silky
The three qualifying scores you receive in obedience competition are also called "legs."

has an added feature, asking your Silky to lie down on your command. The stay exercises are also more difficult, as the time is increased, and you will be asked to walk out of sight while your Silky performs the exercise. Scoring is again based on deductions using the same qualifications as the Novice class. If your Silky receives three qualifying scores, he will earn the title of Companion Dog Excellent, or CDX.

Utility Obedience

Utility competition is for the serious obedience exhibitor. This class combines off-leash heeling with hand signals, and no verbal communication between you and your Silky is allowed during an exercise. Utility also has exercises that work with scent discrimination, retrieving, and jumps, all on your hand signals. A Silky Terrier who earns his Utility Degree, or UD, is a Silky that takes his job seriously!

Therapy Dogs

Silky Terriers have an amazing ability to win over many of the people they meet. Their soft, silky coat is soothing to touch, and their compact, yet sturdy body makes them well suited for lap duty! If your Silky Terrier has begun to master basic obedience exercises, you might want to consider sending him on the career path to becoming a therapy dog.

Silky Terriers can excel in obedience competitions, too!

certified therapy dog. Therapy Dogs, International uses most of the AKC requirements in their test, but adds distractions that might commonly be found in hospitals or adult care facilities as well. If your Silky succeeds and becomes a therapy dog, he will be welcome in schools, hospitals, and nursing homes, where you can share the joy of living with a Silky Terrier.

Agility Competition

The sport of agility is the natural job for your Silky Terrier to enjoy. Agility is rapidly becoming the most popular canine sport, and it offers your Silky a chance to use his quick responses, combining them with his intelligence and zest for activity, and channeling it into one fast-moving game! It also offers both you and your Silky a way to stay active together.

Canine Good Citizen

If your Silky has earned his novice Rally title, he is probably ready to take the AKC Canine Good Citizen exam. If your Silky passes, earning the title CGC for Canine Good Citizen, he has almost all of the qualifications necessary to become a therapy dog.

The CGC test is a series of ten exercises designed to show that your Silky is a well-adjusted, trained companion. A passing grade indicates that your Silky can accept being near strangers and other dogs, accepts being groomed, has learned basic obedience commands, and that you have control of your Silky during the exam.

Once he is known as a "good citizen," you can explore moving up the ladder and becoming a

TIP

Canine Good Citizen Requirements
Here are the exercises your Silky must learn in order to pass his CGC test:
- ✔ Accepting a Friendly Stranger
- ✔ Sitting Politely for Petting
- ✔ Accepting Grooming
- ✔ Walk on a Loose Lead
- ✔ Walk Quietly Through a Crowd
- ✔ Sit and Down on Command and Stay in Place
- ✔ Come When Called
- ✔ Behave Around Other Dogs
- ✔ Behave Around Distractions
- ✔ Accept Separation from Owner

Agility competition is an athletic event in which you and your Silky will complete an obstacle course within a specified amount of time. Sounds easy, right? Those obstacles might include tunnels (a natural for your Silky Terrier), jumps, poles, A-frames, and tables. In AKC competition, there are two classes: Standard class, with obstacles that your Silky must walk on or over; and the Jumpers with Weaves class, which includes only tunnels, jumps, and weave poles. Scoring is a combination of your Silky's time to complete the course, as well as the number of faults on the course for mistakes.

Within the two classes, there are several divisions based on the level of experience. Novice is for the first-time Silky and his owner, and once you and your Silky gain experience by completing the Novice title, you can move up to complete the Open, Excellent, and Master titles. Silky Terriers often excel at agility, and the Master Agility Championship Title, or MACH, is not out of reach for some!

The American Kennel Club also offers a Preferred Division with lower jump heights. Competing in the Preferred Division is a great place to start for an older Silky Terrier, or one that may have trouble negotiating jumps.

You may also have agility events in your area sponsored by the North American Dog Agility Council, or NADAC. These events are similar to the American Kennel Club events, and offer a second venue for you to compete with your Silky Terrier.

Going to Ground— Earthdog Events

Earthdog events begin with an initial introduction to your Silky's quarry, usually rats. If he

"goes to ground," a ten foot tunnel with one right turn leading to a cage of rats, he has passed his IQ test!

Titles are earned in three different Earthdog levels—Junior, Senior, and Master—each with increasing levels of difficulty. Earthdog tests are now open to Silky Terriers, and curious Silky owners have taken advantage of this new event.

Tracking Terriers

When you think of tracking dogs, you probably think of Bloodhounds on the trail of a missing person or criminal. All dogs are equipped with a nose that can discriminate scents, and your Silky is no exception. Silkys can be taught to track; however, that beautiful coat you have worked so hard to maintain may suffer!

THE SENIOR SILKY

As time goes by, your Silky settles into her golden years. A little slower, not quite as sharp, she has earned her senior status.

The Silky Terrier as a whole is blessed with healthy genetics. Add the additional benefits of the great nutrition you have provided, and you have a breed that enjoys an average life expectancy of 12 years or more.

Your Silky is considered to be a senior when she celebrates her ninth birthday. The Silky Terrier generally ages gracefully, and you may not notice any significant changes in your Silky's day-to-day behavior and attitude. Although she might not show it, she is experiencing the normal metabolic changes that are the process of aging.

The Changes Over Time

Suddenly, her lively gait is just a bit slower. She doesn't seem to spot those birds quite as

A senior Silky should be able to enjoy each new day.

readily as in her youth. And she doesn't alert you to every leaf blowing in the wind, as she no longer hears them. Your Silky spends more time enjoying those naps and less time patrolling her home.

Every Silky Terrier ages differently. So how do you know what is normal behavior for the senior Silky? There are no easy answers, and for many Silkys and their owners, the geriatric period is the most difficult period of time for both to enjoy.

The normal aging process brings about subtle changes. For some senior Silkys, no real adjustment to her routine is needed. She will continue to be that little watchdog, alert and ready, and while she is a bit older, she still has a spring in her step and a zest for life. For some other Silkys, time is not as kind. She may feel achy on some days, and have difficulty getting up or maintaining her posture to eliminate.

Keep Them Comfortable

In return for all your Silky has given you, learning to recognize some of the common senior setbacks and knowing how you can help your senior Silky is a great way to be able to give back to her in her remaining years. In many cases, you may be able to provide relief for discomfort, manage her decreased mobility, and help her compensate for her failing senses. At this time in your Silky's life, your goal should be to help her enjoy each day, continuing to have a good quality of life.

Oops—Potty Troubles Again

Perhaps the most common complaint from senior Silky owners is that their previously housebroken Silky starts to eliminate in the house on occasion. Most of the time these lapses begin as infrequent accidents, and the owners believe that the mistakes are just the result of their Silky "getting old." While some decrease in bladder tone may be attributed to normal aging, urine accidents can also be a symptom of many other health concerns that affect the senior Silky Terrier. If your Silky's water consumption has also increased, urine production will be elevated, increasing the risk for urine mistakes. A trip to your veterinarian to rule out organ failure or urinary tract infection is important.

Stool accidents can be anticipated if your Silky is suffering from any spinal trouble or digestive upsets in her golden years. Foods that were once loved and easily tolerated may now cause a breakdown in potty habits, as your Silky's digestive tract can no longer manage those delicacies.

Senile Silkys

Your Silky may require more frequent trips outside to eliminate. It is not uncommon to find that she is now unable to remain clean and dry for long periods of time. If, however, her potty habits have had an overall decline, and your veterinarian cannot find any evidence of an organ function problem or infection, your Silky may be suffering from senility, or cognitive dysfunction syndrome. Cognitive dysfunction is not uncommon in elderly Silkys, but often goes undiagnosed.

There are several symptoms of cognitive dysfunction that the owners notice but do not recognize as anything other than normal aging. The most common is a lapse in housebreaking. Your Silky may also seem confused at times, staring blankly or barking at walls, furniture, or sometimes at nothing at all. She may also be confused as to the time of day, sleeping during the daylight hours and remaining awake and restless at night. Senile Silkys also may begin to snap at family members, as they become startled easily.

Senior Nutritional Needs

The senior Silky has a special set of nutritional requirements to help her look and feel her best each day. When fed a diet formulated for senior dogs, one that has moderate levels of protein, phosphorous, and sodium, the senior Silky has a tool that can help her body slow down the process of aging.

Senior Silkys benefit from a diet that has dietary fiber which can be easily digested by a digestive tract that is moving slower than in her prime years. Fatty acids are as important now as they were in puppyhood for boosting your Silky's immune function and helping her body maintain skin and coat health. Senior diets are often smaller in size, making them much easier for your Silky to chew and digest. Unfortunately, the smaller-sized kibble does not provide the same tartar control action as her larger-sized adult food did, so her oral hygiene may begin to suffer.

Senior diets may also contain slightly increased levels of fat to increase palatability. As your Silky has grown older, her sense of smell may be decreasing. Her appetite is directly affected by her ability to smell her dinner, and the added fat level helps to make it smell and taste better. If your Silky ate dry kibble readily as an adult, but now sniffs it and walks away, you might consider adding a small amount of a senior canned food and warm water to help stimulate her appetite.

Super-sized Seniors

Obesity is a preventable problem that can affect your adult Silky Terrier at any age, but it is most debilitating in the older Silky. If your Silky is carrying a few additional pounds in her early adult years, by the time she reaches senior

Moderate exercise each day will keep your senior Silky from becoming overweight.

TIP

Creature Comforts

Many aging Silky Terriers have to change their routines to offset aging.

Here are some ways to provide a little "extra" comfort:

✔ An old pillow, covered with a waterproof cover and case, makes an inexpensive and washable new bed.

✔ Ramps can be purchased to give your Silky access to furniture if she is reluctant or unable to jump.

✔ Hand signals can be taught or reinforced with basic commands for those Silkys who have hearing loss.

Senior Silky Terriers often age with grace and beauty.

have a super-sized Silky. Genetics may also play a role in obesity, but to a lesser degree than calories and exercise.

Prevention is the Best Medicine

If your Silky is already overweight as an adult, she is less likely to want to exercise as a senior citizen. Obesity also predisposes her to the likelihood that she will suffer from one or more of several other diseases. Excess weight also makes normal aging more difficult for your Silky when it compounds the physical deficits associated with aging.

Prevention is really the key to obesity. To help your senior Silky shed those extra pounds, take a good look at the amount of food you are feeding her each day. Most senior Silkys do not need any more calories than are in two-thirds to a cup of a quality senior diet. Add in the calories of any treats she is receiving and decide whether you should decrease the amount of food or treats she gets each day. You will also need to increase her activity by making sure she gets a short walk each day. Increase her exercise, decrease her caloric intake, and slowly, but surely, her weight will decrease.

The Aches and Pains of Aging

The process of aging is difficult for both you and your Silky. Her immune system works hard to fight off disease, but unfortunately, organ function weakens over time, and her body no longer can hope to win the battle.

Some geriatric health problems can be cured with help from your veterinarian. Other health problems associated with aging cannot be cured, only controlled, and the effects of the disease on your Silky Terrier minimized.

status, those two or three extra pounds may have doubled. Three extra pounds on a Silky Terrier can be equated to fifty extra pounds on the average person. Imagine how difficult life can be carrying that much extra weight if you are healthy, and now imagine it on a senior citizen!

Obesity is the result of a combination of factors and can be easily prevented with a little thought from you. Feeding a Silky more food than her body truly needs to maintain her lifestyle is one factor. Combine too many calories with a decrease in the amount of exercise your senior Silky has on a daily basis, and you

Diabetes

If your Silky Terrier is overweight as an adult, she is more likely to suffer from diabetes mellitus as a senior. Diabetes is a manageable condition caused by an inability of your Silky's pancreas to produce adequate levels of insulin. This deficiency results in abnormally high blood glucose levels, and if left untreated, can result in chronic infections, cataracts, and eventual death.

Diabetes is often not recognized right away, although its symptoms are easy to identify in the older Silky. A cloudy appearance to the eyes, the result of cataracts, is often the first thing the owners of a diabetic Silky notice. The diabetic Silky may have been drinking more water than normal and urinating more frequently, but the owner attributes these symptoms to the aging process. Diabetic Silky Terriers will often eat ravenously, seeming to be unable to satisfy their appetite, and yet they appear to be losing weight.

Diabetes mellitus cannot be cured; however, the disease can be managed with a carefully controlled diet and insulin injections given at each meal. Regulating your Silky's blood glucose will be done with the help of your veterinarian, by monitoring her glucose level over time. Once the disease is regulated, the diabetic Silky Terrier can continue to lead a normal, active life.

Musculoskeletal Maladies

The loss of muscle mass that accompanies normal aging may have no negative effect on your senior Silky. This loss of muscle function can be a problem when it is combined with a number of orthopedic problems that result from your Silky's senior status.

Degenerative joint disease is common in the senior Silky. As your Silky's body ages normally,

it can no longer produce enough synovial fluid to maintain the proper lubrication for the body's various joints. As synovial fluid in her knees, hips, shoulders, and spine decreases, the surrounding cartilage deteriorates, causing the joints to move less effectively, often with bone-on-bone contact. Stiffness upon rising and temporary lameness can be early indications that your Silky's joints are not functioning normally due to the aging process.

As degenerative joint disease progresses, movement of the joint becomes less effective, and the joint itself becomes inflamed. Inflammation of the joint is known as arthritis. Arthritis is a common, painful condition found in the senior Silky. Arthritis may cause constant stiffness, making your Silky reluctant to move around. If severe arthritis is present, your Silky may be in so much pain that she attempts to bite if touched or moved.

Arthritic Silkys may be very reluctant to exercise, yet this is important to keep the joints from becoming stiffer and helps to stimulate the production of synovial fluid. If your Silky is arthritic and overweight, the combination of too much weight on painful joints may be prohibiting her from truly enjoying her remaining quality of life.

There have been significant improvements made in veterinary medicine with regard to orthopedic pain, offering you a variety of options to help your Silky feel more comfortable. Nonsteroidal anti-inflammatory medications aimed at reducing discomforts are readily available from your veterinarian. These medications are safe and effective when used as directed.

Alternative medicine has also given us neutraceuticals such as glucosamine, chondroitin, and other products aimed at helping your Silky's own body produce synovial fluid. Chiropractic care, acupuncture, and hydrotherapy are all alternative medicine options that may benefit your Silky if she has a debilitating orthopedic condition.

Dental Disease

As your Silky has matured, those pearly white teeth of puppyhood have become just a bit more yellowed and dull over time. Your veterinarian may have used ultrasonic scaling and polishing to help minimize decay through adulthood, but over time, your Silky's dental health will continue to decline. As an elderly Silky, she will begin to lose teeth and may suffer bone loss from decay. Her appetite may also decline if chewing becomes uncomfortable.

Dental hygiene in your Silky's golden years requires your special attention. Bacteria in her mouth from decaying teeth, plaque, and tartar have a direct pathway to affect your Silky's circulatory system. Her immune system, once strong and powerful, has to work much harder now, and even the smallest amount of bacteria from her mouth can have a dramatic, negative affect on her kidneys and other organs.

Regularly scheduled dental cleanings at your veterinarian are a must in your Silky's senior years. Antibiotic therapy may also be beneficial

━━━━━━━━━━ T I P ━━━━━━━━━━

Senior Medication
Never give human medications to your Silky Terrier.

Anti-inflammatory drugs that are used in humans are not the same as those used in veterinary medicine and can cause bleeding disorders and organ failure.

Always consult with your veterinarian before beginning any medication.

in reducing the risk of infection from dental disease as your Silky continues to age.

Cardiac Concerns

A properly functioning cardiovascular system is vital if your Silky Terrier is going to enjoy those activities she has gotten so good at. Silkys enjoy longevity, but along with a longer life span comes the likelihood of cardiac disease. Cardiac disease, also called congestive heart failure, is a decline or inability of the heart to function properly. A diminished cardiac output means slower circulation of blood. Slower circulation means more difficulty maintaining normal oxygenation through the respiratory system. Decreased blood flow means increased waste products in the bloodstream, resulting in an overload on your Silky's kidneys and liver. Poor cardiac function has an effect on almost every other organ in your Silky Terrier's body.

Congestive heart failure often begins with a slight decrease in your Silky's activity level. As the heart has to work harder to pump blood through the circulatory system, your Silky may begin to cough at times, especially when excited. In advanced cases, your Silky may begin to appear "potbellied" as her abdomen fills with fluid, the result of a circulatory system that can no longer keep up the workload.

Good-bye, My Friend

Saying good-bye is never easy. It is always our hope and wish that our beloved elderly Silky will one day drift off to sleep on her favorite bed, and quietly slip away to a better place. A natural passing can be peaceful, but does not help to ease the grief you will experience at losing such a dear companion.

All too often, we are forced to watch our Silky deteriorate slowly, her quality of life decreasing with each day that passes. Advancing in age, increasingly more uncomfortable, and unable to truly express her pain, you may have to consider whether it is the right time to help ease your Silky's pain by considering humane euthanasia.

Euthanasia is a personal decision. It is never a decision that is considered to be easy, nor one that a Silky owner wants to make in haste. But for many owners, the pain of watching their Silky suffer is greater than the grief that making the decision and losing her will bring. They want to remember their Silky in her best years, chasing rabbits, barking at neighbors, and exhibiting that terrier exuberance.

Euthanasia is a single injection of an anesthetic given intravenously. It is a quick and painless procedure, taking little more than seconds to be effective. As the injection is administered, your Silky will quite literally "go to sleep," breathing a bit heavier as the sedation takes effect, and finally, will peacefully take her last breath. The ability to end your Silky's suf-

My best friend, my Silky Terrier.

fering in a dignified, peaceful manner is the ultimate way to tell her that you loved her!

The Grieving Process

Grief is a normal part of healing following the loss of your beloved Silky Terrier. There is no right way to grieve, nor a normal length of time to feel a sense of loss. Each individual grieves in his or her own way, remembering good times and mourning the loss.

Following the loss of your Silky, you may choose to add another to your home. For some, the grieving process includes the addition of another Silky Terrier as quickly as possible. For others, the thought of trying to replace the one they have lost causes more heartache. No two Silky Terriers are alike! There may be another Silky Terrier in your future, but it will never replace the one that first captured your heart.

INFORMATION

Breed Clubs and Kennel Clubs

American Kennel Club (AKC)
Registration
5580 Centerview Drive
Raleigh, NC 27606-3390
www.akc.org

Silky Terrier Club of America
www.silkyterrierclubofamerica.org

Health-related Information

Canine Eye Registration Foundation (CERF)
625 Harrison Street
Purdue University
W. Lafayette, IN 47907-2026
Phone: 765-494-8179
Fax: 765-494-9981
www.vmdb.org

Orthopedic Foundation for Animals (OFA)
2300 E. Nifong Boulevard
Columbia, Missouri 65201-3806
Phone: 573-442-0418
Fax: 573-875-5073
www.offa.org

Microchip/Pet Registries

American Kennel Club (AKC)
Companion Animal Recovery
5580 Centerview Drive, Suite 250
Raleigh, NC 27606-3389
24-Hour Recovery Hotline: 1-800-252-7894
www.akccar.org

Avid Microchip I.D. Systems
78294 Oak Ridge Road
Folsom, LA 70437
Phone: 1-800-434-2843
www.avidmicrochip.com

Home Again Pet Recovery Service
P.O. Box 2014
East Syracuse, NY 13057-4514
Phone: 1-866-PETID24
www.homeagainid.com

National Dog Registry
P.O. Box 116
Woodstock, NY 12498-0116
Phone: 1-800-NDR-DOGS
www.nationaldogregistry.com

Periodicals

The Silky Terrier Times
Norma Baugh, Editor
11203 Jones Road West
Houston, TX 77065
www.geocities.com/silkyterriertimes

*The American Kennel Club Family Dog
Magazine*
Phone: 1-800-490-5675
www.akc.org/pubs/familydog

The American Kennel Club Gazette Magazine
Phone: 1-800-533-7323
www.akc.org/pubs/gazette

Dog Fancy/Dog World
P.O. Box 6050
Mission Viejo, CA 92690-6050
Phone: 1-800-896-4939
www.dogchannel.com/dog/magazines

Recommended Reading

Hingeley, Marshall and Wren. *Silky Terriers
Today.* New York, NY: Howell Book House,
1996.

Retired show dogs can make excellent pets!

Smith, Peggy. *The Complete Silky Terrier.* New York, NY: Howell Book House, 1990.

Tennant, Colin. *Breaking Bad Habits in Dogs.* Barron's Educational Series, Inc., Hauppauge, NY, 2003.

Benjamin, Carol Lea. *Second Hand Dog—How to Turn Yours Into a First Rate Pet.* Indianapolis, IN: John Wiley and Sons, 1998.

Miller, Pat. *The Power of Positive Dog Training.* New York, NY: Howell Book House, 2001.

Coile, Caroline. *Show Me! A Dog Showing Primer.* Barron's Educational Series, Inc., Hauppauge, NY, 1997.

The Monks of New Skete. *The Art of Raising a Puppy.* New York, NY: Little Brown and Co., 1991.

Web Sites

Silky Terrier Resourse
www.silkyterrier.net

The Association of Pet Dog Trainers (APDT)
www.apdt.com

National Association of Dog Obedience Instructors (NADOI)
www.nadoi.org

Dog Trainer Search
www.dogtrainersearch.com

North American Dog Agility Council (NADAC)
www.nadac.com

Therapy Dogs International (TDI)
www.tdi-dog.org

■INDEX

About the Author

Brenda Belmonte's love of dogs began over 20 years ago. She continues to participate with multiple breeds in both conformation and obedience dog shows throughout the United States. She is a Judges Educational Instructor for the Pug Dog Club of America, and an experienced all-breed obedience instructor. Brenda is the owner of a dog training business in Illinois and has been the practice manager for a veterinary clinic for 20 years. She specializes in behavior and nutrition, and provides guidance and behavioral services to new puppy owners. She is a breed columnist for the *AKC Gazette* and *Pug Talk Magazine*. Brenda is also the author of *The Pug Handbook* by Barron's Educational Series, Inc.

Cover Photos

Front, inside front, back, and inside back covers: Isabelle Francais.

Photo Credits

Isabelle Francais: pages 2–3, 4, 12, 13, 15, 16, 18, 19, 21, 23, 27, 29, 31, 33, 36, 38, 41 (top and bottom), 45, 46, 48, 49, 56, 62, 66, 67, 69, 70, 71, 72, 74, 75, 78, 79, 82, 84, 88, 91, 93; Kent Dannen: 5, 6, 7 (top right, bottom), 11, 20, 22, 25, 28, 30, 40, 47, 50, 52, 57, 61, 76, 80, 85, 87; Cheryl Ertelt: 37, 44, 54; Tara Darling: 55; Norvia Behling: 7 (top left).

Important Note

The Silky Terrier was first described to me as "not just another toy dog." They are smart, inquisitive and always capable of making their owners think. Anyone who has had the pleasure of owning a Silky will tell you how much they enjoy living with them. Their upbeat personality, "big dog" attitude, and devotion to their family, make them one of the dog world's best kept secrets.

Throughout, the book alternates gender for each chapter.

Dedication

This book is dedicated to the Silky Terrier breeder, whose love of the breed has had an impact on the preservation of this wonderful little dog. I would like to extend special thanks to those Silky owners and breeders who so willingly answered my many questions.

All inquiries should be addressed to:
Barron's Educational Series, Inc.
250 Wireless Boulevard
Hauppauge, NY 11788
www.barronseduc.com

ISBN-13: 978-0-7641-3537-8
ISBN-10: 0-7641-3537-6

Library of Congress Catalog Card No. 2006016405

Library of Congress Cataloging-in-Publication Data
Belmonte, Brenda.
    Silky terriers : everything about purchase, grooming, health, nutrition, care, and training / Brenda Belmonte ; filled with full color photographs ; illustrations by Michele Earle-Bridges.
        p. cm. — (A complete pet owner's manual)
    Includes bibliographical references and index.
    ISBN-13: 978-0-7641-3537-8 (alk. paper)
    ISBN-10: 0-7641-3537-6 (alk. paper)
    1. Silky terriers. I. Title. II. Series.

SF429.S66B45 2007
636.76—dc22   2006016405

Printed in China
9 8 7 6 5 4 3 2